'NOT SO BARREN O

Tony Lurcock grew up in Kent and was educated at Oxford. He became lecturer in English at Helsinki University, and subsequently at Åbo Akademi. He returned to Oxford for research, and taught there, and in America, until his recent retirement.

Arrival in Turku, nineteenth century

'Not So Barren or Uncultivated'

BRITISH TRAVELLERS IN FINLAND
1760–1830

Tony Lurcock

'He then directed his course for Abo in Finland,
where there is nothing that pleased him in the survey,
or can amuse by the description . . . He found the
province of Finland, however, not so barren or
uncultivated as he had been taught to expect.'
Critical Review (1775)

First published in 2010
by CB editions
146 Percy Road London W12 9QL
www.cbeditions.com

Front cover: *Viewing the Midnight Sun. TORNAO IN LAPLAND.*
Engraving by Thomas Bewick; frontispiece of Matthew Consett's *A Tour
through Sweden, Swedish Lapland, Finland and Denmark*, 1789.

Printed in England by Imprint Digital, Exeter EX5 5HY

ISBN 978-0-9561073-9-8

Contents

Acknowledgements

Composing this book has been largely a solitary activity, carried out over several decades, with many long periods of inattention. It is probable that I have forgotten some of the people who have given help or advice along the way, and very probable that several such people have forgotten that they ever helped or advised.

The following have certainly given help at different times and places, in matters both literary and technical: Ben Goluboff, Tim Griggs, Bill Mead, Bernard O'Donoghue, Simon Rae, David Ripley, Roger Sell, Katherine Turner and David Wilson. On the home front my sons, Pontus and Casper, have been the book's allies in several areas: typing out more than a hundred thousand words onto a computer, maintaining and explaining the said computer, helping with all sorts of word-processing problems, and offering advice on content and style.

My friend Silvester Mazzarella has stuck with me and with the project since the beginning, reading and commenting on numerous drafts, and always leaving me feeling that it was all worthwhile. As the book headed for publication Jonathan Clark sorted out various word-processing problems, and masterminded the production of the map and frontispiece.

I thank Dominique Enright for proof-reading, and Charles Boyle for expertise in matters of design and production.

Any comments, corrections or additions would be welcomed by the author at 9 Monmouth Road, Oxford OX1 4TD, UK, or by email to tonylurcock@yahoo.com.

Place Names in Swedish and Finnish

(Archaic Swedish spellings are in parentheses.)

Björneborg	Pori
Borgå (Bergo)	Porvoo
Brahestad	Raahe
Elsing (Helsing)	Helsinki (village)
Enontekis	Enontekiö
Fredrikshamn	Hamina
Gamla Karleby	Kokkola
Helsingfors	Helsinki
Lovisa (Louisa)	Loviisa
Ny Karleby	Uusikaarlepyy
Nyslott	Savonlinna
Peterlax	Pyterlahti
Pyttis	Pyhtää
Sibho	Sibbo
Sveaborg	Suomenlinna
Tammerfors (Tamerfers)	Tampere
Tourneå	Tornio
Uleåborg	Oulu
Vasa	Vaasa
Åbo	Turku
Övertourneå	Ylitornio

Preface

This book has its origins in occasional talks given to Finnish-British Societies in various towns in Finland some forty years ago. They were readings rather than lectures, and offered striking and amusing extracts from books by British travellers in Finland. Over the years I have found many more books, and discovered a good deal about many of the writers.

Viewed chronologically these accounts arrange themselves in a developing pattern. In the eighteenth century Finland was a destination almost exclusively for those who were rich and titled, as well as bold and adventurous. With the coming of the steamboats, first on the Baltic, and later from England, sightseers from a different class of society appeared, and by the end of the nineteenth century ladies as well as gentlemen were taking leisurely tours of Finland, especially in the lake district. The twentieth century saw visitors of all classes travelling to Finland, often interested in the politics and social institutions of this new republic, and attracted also because it was unbelievably cheap. The present volume covers the earliest part of this history, from the 1760s to the 1830s.

All of the books which are discussed and cited are by English or Scottish authors, and were published in Britain. The book has two limitations: I have made no attempt to compare British travellers with, for example, those from Germany or France, nor have I (with one exception) made use of or sought out unpublished material. The presentation is broadly chronological, but I have put a few writers a little out of sequence where I have felt that this would make the book more cohesive.

The book is first and foremost an anthology. The extracts are chosen from a score or more of accounts, with a short introduction to each writer. I have attempted to make the book more than a chronology by linking some of the recurrent features, ranging from the writers' often rudimentary ethnological instincts to their opinions of the roads and post-houses. There is not always a great deal of consensus: every traveller tells his own tale. It is amusing rather then bewildering to find, for example, how some of them considered that crossing from Finland to Russia was to move from civilisation to savagery, while others held the opposite opinion.

In the Introduction I have presented the writers against the background of their times, describing some of the cultural, social and literary ideas which they reflect. Themes such as 'the picturesque' can then be mentioned in the body of the book without further digression. It is by no means necessary to read the introduction to enjoy the contents of the book, nor need the book be read chronologically, in full, or indeed at all. That is the way with anthologies.

The earliest accounts of Finland often confuse the races: Swedes, Finns and 'Lapps'. In particular travellers in Lapland did not usually distinguish Finns living in Lapland from what are now known as Sami, the native inhabitants. The term Finlander is commonly used where we should now say Finn, but Swedish-speaking Finns, confusingly for modern readers, are often referred to as 'Swedes'.

Several writers describe their journeys west of St Petersburg as passing 'through Russian Finland'. This phrase, like references to 'the Governor of Russian Finland', is a reminder that the map of Finland has for two and a half centuries been periodically redrawn. The eastern border had been moved west by the Peace of Turku in 1743; the Kymijoki, with its famous bridge, marked the border between what travellers usually termed Swedish Finland and Russian Finland, and Hamina became the Russian garrison town. This border remained until Russia occupied Finland in 1808–9; by the Treaty of Hamina (1809) all of Finland was ceded by Sweden to Russia. Finland was not incorporated into Russia, but became an autonomous Grand Duchy, keeping the constitution and legal system from the Swedish era. At the Diet of Porvoo (1809) the Czar undertook to uphold the Lutheran faith and 'the constitutional laws and rights' of Finland; Finns swore allegiance to the Czar. Finnish Karelia and the province of Vyborg (Viipuri in Finnish) were now part of the Grand Duchy, and travellers did not reach Russia proper until they were almost in sight of St Petersburg. This border remained until the Second World War. For travellers, as for most inhabitants, these changes of sovereignty had little effect at this time; they are mentioned here to make better sense of incidental allusions in the text, and to avoid confusion about where Finland's borders actually were.

The problems of place names are not so easily addressed. Firstly, travellers mention many places whose names bear no resemblance to anything that can be found on accessible maps of Finland. This may be because they are Swedish names which have long been replaced by Finnish ones, or because they are the writers' phonetic approximations to what they thought they heard; on occasion it could be both of these, presumably. In the quotations I have let the names stand as published, but in my own text I have given the modern, Finnish names to all places that I have identified; the others are indicated by quotation marks. A more troublesome matter has been that of Swedish and Finnish place names. Almost without exception writers until the end of the nineteenth century used Swedish names: Helsingfors rather than Helsinki, Åbo rather than Turku, and Nyslott rather than Savonlinna. I don't think that there is any satisfactory way out of this difficulty, so I have adopted what seems to be the least unsatisfactory option: instead of pestering the text with a succession of alternative names, I have kept place names unaltered in the quoted passages – nearly always the Swedish version – and used the current Finnish names in my own text. Readers unfamiliar with the Swedish names may need to refer to the list of place names, but the context will usually make things clear.

I should mention too that I have kept the spelling of the original texts, and am fairly confident that all apparent misspellings are actually original. A few very obvious misprints and significant mistakes in punctuation have been silently corrected. Modern readers may be as amused at the English attempts to render Finnish place names, as English travellers a century later were by Finnish attempts to produce a restaurant menu in English.

The Appendix contains some material which would have clogged up the narrative, but which seemed to me worth preserving. The Notes are mostly page references for the quoted passages. I have avoided the distraction of footnotes, or numbers in the text to indicate notes. By these means I hope that the book will be readable as well as accurate.

The present book carries the story down only to the 1830s. Whether further volumes appear will have to depend on the reception of what follows. All that I will say now is that there is more where this came from.

Introduction

Anyone who contemplated travelling to Finland before the last years of the eighteenth century would have found little information beyond the final brief chapter of the *Germania* of the Latin historian Tacitus, written in AD 98. This is how it reads in John Aiken's translation from 1777:

> The Fenni live in a state of amazing savageness and squalid poverty. They are destitute of arms, horses and settled abodes: their food is herbs; their cloathing, skins; their bed, the ground. Their only dependence is on their arrows, which, for want of iron, are headed with bone; and the chace is the support of the women as well as the men, who wander with them in the pursuit, and demand a share of the prey. Nor do they provide any other shelter for their infants from the wild beasts and storms, than a covering of branches twisted together. This is the resort of youth; this is the receptacle of old age.

This description, wrote John Thomas James in 1816, 'is often quoted in allusion to their present habits and character'. Many of the British travellers from the late eighteenth century who published accounts of their experiences in Finland felt that very little had changed in the intervening centuries. Writer after writer recorded discomfort, disgust, and disbelief. Edward Daniel Clarke, crossing from Vartsala to Turku in sub-Arctic temperatures in January 1800, wrote that his journey 'was one of extreme suffering; and perhaps few *English* travellers ever encountered one of greater trial'. 'Yet,' he continued, 'any thing was preferable to remaining in the wretched and unwholesome hovel where we had passed the night.' Like many other early travellers, he found the horrors of the accommodation even worse than the rigours of the Finnish winter. Summer travelling was no less daunting: the bugs indoors and the mosquitoes outdoors caused more distress than the blood-curdling temperatures of winter. 'No one, but those who have suffered,' wrote John Carr, 'could believe them capable of producing so much torment.'

The early travellers found the inhabitants of Finland even less attractive than the country itself. 'Unpolished in their manners, and still retaining the vestiges of Gothic ignorance, they present not many charms to tempt the traveller,' observed Sir Nathaniel Wraxall. 'The manners of the people were so revolting,' wrote Clarke, 'that one hesitates in giving the description of anything so disgusting.' Sir Robert Ker Porter thought that 'their appearance is ten times more savage than the grimmest Russian I ever met', while Andrew Swinton added that 'the Finland women are extremely coarse in their persons and features'. The peasants spoke, in Wraxall's words, 'a barbarous jargon equally unintelligible to a Swede or a Russian'. In the whole country it was only the hardiness of the horses which regularly met with praise. Why, then, did these long-suffering travellers not stay at home, or at least confine their movements to the well-known resorts of 'civilised' Europe?

There were, in fact, all sorts of reasons which prompted British travellers from the mid-eighteenth century onwards to turn their horses' heads to the North. Wraxall was expressing a commonly held view when he wrote in 1775:

Mankind are become more sceptical, and refuse to be amused with superstitious legends, or the wanton sallies of a luxuriant and fertile imagination. The refinement and civilisation of modern manners, has rendered it no difficult matter to inspect kingdoms and provinces, to which access was formerly barred by bigotry, barbarism, and want of all police.

'Fabulous' journeys were coming to be seen as a taste which belonged to an earlier age; it was now more likely to be an empirical urge which sent travellers on their way. Wraxall stressed that the world was now safe enough for people to go to remote countries to find things out for themselves. Arthur de Capell Brooke, who travelled to the North Cape in 1820, sought to correct the 'general notions' that northern Europe suffered 'almost continual darkness' and was mostly 'fast bound . . . in chains of ice':

> A person . . . who can divest himself of those ideas, and meet with cheerfulness the many little inconveniences to which everyone who leaves his own country is liable, will find in the North much to gratify his curiosity, and interest his feelings.

Partly it was novelty which attracted travellers to the north of Europe, and which made their written accounts so popular. From about 1770, as Katherine Turner has shown, book reviewers were complaining that readers were bored with accounts of traditional European travel, and were anxious to read about fresh fields. Changing taste, too, played an important part. Richard Holmes has described this phenomenon:

> Hitherto the English literary traveller (for the great part male, well-heeled and accompanied by guides, valets or tutors) had adhered to a well-defined circuit through Europe and the Levant that over three centuries had become known as the Grand Tour. 'The grand object of travel,' pronounced Dr Johnson, 'is to visit the shores of the Mediterranean . . .' The essential attraction was

3

towards the cities and civilizations of the south. To go north and east – beyond say the international port of Hamburg and the old walled and turreted medieval city of Lübeck, was to journey beyond the pale of Western culture. The shores of the distant Baltic, and the half-legendary lands of the midnight sun beyond, were *terra incognita* for all but a few hardy sailors, merchants, diplomats, and the new race of commercial travellers.

Few travellers in any of these four categories have left any account of their movements in Finland, at least in the period up to about 1830. The published travel books, with only a few exceptions, are by writers who fit Holmes's description of 'the English literary traveller', although it was more commonly the tutor who subsequently published an account. Most writers of this time published their travelogues in the form of a journal or a series of letters; written at the time, these could be easily worked up for publication, and even revisited for a later, expanded edition.

More than novelty was involved: there were sternly practical reasons for travellers to head north. The traditional routes of the Grand Tour were at this time repeatedly obstructed or rendered hazardous by the continental wars – by the French Revolution in 1789 and then, until the Battle of Waterloo in 1814, by Napoleon. 'The angry decrees of renovated war,' wrote Carr in 1805, had 'closed the gates of the south; the north alone lay expanded before me.' Throughout this period young men and their tutors were having to find new directions, and substitutes for the Grand Tour. One was Edinburgh, christened at this time 'the Athens of the North' because of the concentration of educated travellers who had temporarily settled there. Northern Europe was another popular alternative.

The very idea of the traditional Grand Tour, which had

4

become popular after the Restoration, was actually being questioned long before the time of Napoleon. Clarke, himself a Cambridge tutor, and the most significant traveller represented in this volume, called the Grand Tourists' bluff in uncompromising terms; addressing the young nobility of England, he wrote:

> But, let me ask, have your continental expeditions been attended with that advantage, which it is natural to suppose would result from the lavish contribution, both of time and treasure, which has been exacted to complete them? A painful witness to the contrary, it is with deep concern I call to mind, the shameful manner in which they are frequently accomplished. Roaming about the Continent, in almost proverbial apathy, becomes your characteristic. For what purpose do you travel? Is it to associate promiscuously with adventurers? – to be immured in gaming houses? – to be seen all the morning at the billiard table; and all the evening intoxicated; or at the faro bank? – to become the object of contemptuous ridicule in every country you visit? Is it for this Albion pours forth her sons upon foreign ground; and in the vain hope of obtaining ornaments to her senate, honours to her state, understandings enlarged, prejudices corrected, and taste refined?

Few of these traditional dissipations of the English upper class were available in northern Europe, so even when the roads to the south were clear some travellers – and their tutors especially – could still find good reasons for heading north. The earliest traveller represented here, Joseph Marshall, explained how disappointment with his own Grand Tour through France, Italy, Spain and Germany in 1761 had influenced him to try something entirely different:

I soon found that I had spent much time, money and attention, in order to return home, judiciously speaking, as ignorant as I went out. Reflection convinced me, that there were numerous objects, highly deserving attention in each country, which I had passed by without notice; and I regretted a journey performed in the rawness of youth, which afforded me so little instruction.

Many of these early accounts of travel in Finland offer something more, and more important, than a simple change of direction. They imply, and at times express, views of travel which actively reject what Holmes describes as 'the old eighteenth-century idea of the Grand Tour as an extension of classical education and the reverential study of the masterpieces of antiquity'. Matthew Consett, in his own rather naive way, described such a feeling on his return from Lapland in 1786:

> We have beheld human nature under her rudest appearances: we have seen her in a State very different from that which appears in cities or at Courts, and have been enabled to draw conclusions from the varieties of life.

Mary Wollstonecraft offered a more enlightened and empirical view of travel in *Letters Written in Sweden, Norway, and Denmark* (1796):

> If travelling, as the completion of a liberal education, were to be adopted on rational grounds, the northern states ought to be visited before the more polished parts of Europe, to serve as the elements even of the knowledge of manners, only to be acquired by tracing the various shades in different countries.

She suggests here that knowledge of the primitive north should be a prelude to visiting the rest of Europe, so that the traveller could, so to speak, trace the development and advance of civilisation. Clarke shared this view; '[a] view of mankind in their origin opens before me,' he wrote to his Cambridge frined William Otter as he prepared to leave Stockholm for Finland.

Consett was one of many travellers to Finland whose special interest was Lapland, an area where the attractions were as varied as they were legendary. The very name 'Lapland' held for eighteenth-century readers some of the mythological power that Siberia had in later ages, as a place of great remoteness, beyond the boundary of civilised life. There was more than this. The Laplanders had for centuries had a reputation throughout Europe for magical practices and sorcery. In Shakespeare's *Comedy of Errors* a bewildered character exclaims, 'Sure these are but imaginary wiles,/ And Lapland sorcerers inhabit here.' These activities had been described vividly by Joannes Scheffer in his *Lapponia* (1673), published in England as *History of Lapland* in 1674. Fuseli's famous painting *The Night-Hag visiting the Lapland Witches* is dated 1796, while he was an associate of the Royal Academy, and would have been exhibited in London. The magic drum, used as an aid to augury, had long been prohibited in Finland, but seemed to be still a living presence. Clarke wrote that 'the divining-drums, by which fortunes are told by sorcerers, are so well known . . . that it were superfluous to insert a description'. Hundreds of miles south, near the Baltic coast, Porter commented on the 'wild scenery' which was 'the very theatre in which a romance writer would place his supernatural visitants'. As late as 1818 John Keats makes reference to 'a Lapland witch'.

An attraction both more immediate and widespread than witchcraft was the vogue for Northern primitivism in the later eighteenth century. The 'Goths,' writes Barton, 'exercised a growing fascination for the preromantic imagination . . . [T]hey seemed to embody primitive virility, vitality, valour, and hardihood, in contrast to the effete and degenerate Romans of the late Empire, heirs of an overrefined and dying civilisation.' Edward Gibbon had written that '[m]any vestiges attest the ancient residence of the *Goths* in the countries beyond the Baltic'. The literary dimension of the primitive is seen, for example, in the popularity of the Ossian poems, translated and published by James MacPherson in the early 1760s, and of Percy's *Reliques of Ancient English Poetry* (1765). Literary primitivism was seen also in ballad poetry, which was popular long before Wordsworth and Coleridge published their *Lyrical Ballads* in 1798. Wordsworth wrote in 1800 of the 'elementary feelings' found among the rustic poor: he would have found them in abundance in Finland.

Many English readers knew something of Lapland from one of the most popular poems of the century, *The Seasons,* by the Scottish-born poet James Thomson. The passage describing Lapland was added in the edition of 1730.

> Wide o'er the spacious regions of the north,
> That see Boötes urge his tardy wain,
> A boisterous race, by frosty Caurus pierced,
> Who little pleasure know and fear no pain,
> Prolific swarm. They once relumed the flame
> Of lost mankind in polished slavery sunk;
> Drove martial horde on horde, with dreadful sweep
> Resistless rushing o'er the enfeebled south,
> And gave the vanquished world another form.
> Not such the sons of Lapland; wisely they
> Despise the insensate barbarous trade of war;
> They ask no more than simple Nature gives,
> They love their mountains and enjoy their storms.
> No false desires, no pride-created wants,

Disturb the peaceful current of their time,
And through the restless ever-tortured maze
Of pleasure or ambition bid it rage.

(The rest of Thomson's description is printed as Appendix 1.) So many of the travellers of this time actually quote from 'Winter' that it seems likely that it was influential in popularising Lapland.

Thomson's chief sources were Scheffer's *History of Lapland*, and Maupertuis's *Figure of the Earth*, published in English in 1738 (the author had been sent to Lapland by Louis XV to measure the length of a degree of the meridian). Thomson was fascinated by their descriptions of the Arctic nights, the fairy-land enchantments, the brightness of the stars, and hunting by the light of 'meteors' – a contemporary term for the Aurora Borealis. Joseph Addison often refers to Lapland in *The Spectator*; in two numbers from 1712 poetry from Lapland is introduced:

> The following Verses are a Translation of a *Lapland* Love-Song, which I met with in *Scheffer's* History of that Country. I was agreeably surpriz'd to find a Spirit of Tenderness and Poetry in a region which I have never suspected for delicacy.

It seemed to the writer astonishing that lyrics 'not unworthy old *Greece* or *Rome*' should be produced in a climate so dark and cold that ''tis amazing that the poor Natives shou'd get food, or be tempted to propagate their Species'. (See Appendix 2 for the text of the poems.)

Such was the vogue for Lapland that Consett, arriving in Tornio in 1786, was told by a resident, Professor Helands, that 'many Englishmen had visited Tornao in his time, and [he] shewed us Letters he had received from persons of rank in London'. By the end of the century, writes Herbert Hartman,

'Lapland . . . was becoming an item (was Maupertuis to blame?) in the Romantics' paraphernalia of remoteness.' In English Augustan poetry Lapland became established as a place of unsullied and romantic isolation. Nowhere could be imagined as further from the dark satanic mills. Words alone could not do justice to these Finnish scenes; several of the writers embellished their accounts with engravings, and these were occasionally issued separately in portfolios.

In the dawn of the Romantic Movement it is hardly surprising to find travellers seeking new manifestations of the picturesque. The theory of the picturesque – 'views seen as being artistic but containing elements of wildness and irregularity' – was promoted by William Gilpin and Uvedale Price in the later eighteenth century. Wraxall was one of the travellers who rather self-consciously relished the picturesque, as in this summer vignette from the Åland Islands:

> Many of the prospects were, however, so wondrously picturesque and romantic, that I frequently stopped the boatmen for a minute, to gaze upon the extraordinary scene around me.

In winter, too, there was much to appreciate: William Coxe, arriving in Finland in early February, enjoyed 'the picturesque appearance of the sledge team'. Clarke went far beyond a scientist's appraisal of the landscape, echoing Augustan poets like Thomson and Joseph Warton in praising the grandeur of the 'prospects'; the sketches which he made in Lapland, some of them later engraved, 'were always picturesque'.

Some of the travellers to northern Europe were surprised to find that they had discovered a race of people who seemed to be untouched by European civilisation. This was the very opposite of what was either sought or felt by travellers to Italy and Greece. Thomson had perhaps prepared a way by idealising the Laplanders as a peace-loving people, perfectly in tune with nature. The Lapland passage in *The Seasons* reveals interests which go far beyond the picturesque: Thomson presents an aspect of primitivism which puts forward a progressivist view of history. The scenes he depicts are inhabited by virtuous primitives – noble savages, no less – who substantiated ideas developed by Voltaire and Rousseau. 'In his native Switzerland,' writes Barton, 'Rousseau found a new Arcadia, where a sturdy peasantry, uncorrupted by the evils of civilisation, lived simple and virtuous lives amid natural surroundings inspiring in their awesome grandeur.' Several British travellers found this new Arcadia in Lapland.

Curiosity about primitive civilisation is seen frequently in the following pages. John Bowring considered that no nation could have been more untouched than Finland:

> The history of a people not very numerous, but very widely scattered, inhabiting a frigid and inhospitable climate, is in truth soon told, and the vicissitudes of sovereignty, the change of masters, affect this race of man almost as little as they affect the wolves, whose troops occupy their magnificent pine-tree forests, or the seals that play about the borders of the Bothnian Sea.

The primitiveness of the inhabitants of Lapland aroused the curiosity and caught the imagination of many travellers. Consett wrote:

> Ignorant of all the improvements of Life, unknowing in the several embellishments of society, they live, in the interior parts of Lapland, as much as possible in a state of Nature.

Several travellers expressed their surprise at finding any signs of civilisation at all.

The State of Nature was a concept which greatly exercised some eighteenth-century thinkers. Samuel Johnson had travelled to the Hebrides in 1773, taking, as Mary Lascelles writes, 'the opportunity to observe living people still tracing a pattern of life elsewhere extinct, one which he had hitherto apprehended only through the historical imagination.' It was on this Scottish tour that Johnson and Boswell discussed taking a journey through the Baltic; Johnson felt, presumably, that further north this 'pattern of life' could be experienced in an even more unspoiled form. It was Boswell, not Johnson, who had a change of heart.

It was in Lapland, rather than around the Baltic, that such a way of life could best be viewed. Brooke quotes the opinion of Vaillant ('well known for his travels in Africa, and who has had favourable opportunities of observing man in the state of nature in which savages exist') that 'in an uncivilised state, man is naturally good'. Brooke describes an episode among the 'Finlanders' at Jarhois, south of Muonio, where three young men 'in a state of perfect nudity' from the sauna entered the room where he and his party were sitting and the women ('themselves very slightly attired') were spinning:

> A stranger from far more civilised parts of the world than Finland is greatly surprised at finding the intercourse between the sexes so unconstrained and yet so innocent.

Episodes such as this caused several travellers of this era to consider, and even reassess, what the term 'civilised' implied. It was not only in the 'state of nature' that such behaviour was noted: Clarke devotes a whole page to describing how a trusting merchant in Oulu discounted a large bill without any security – an instance of 'unmixed virtue'.

Combined with this idealisation of the people in Finland is a discomposing counter-movement of colourful denigration, already described; Clarke likened a Lapp to the 'long-lost link between man and ape'. '[A] curious ambivalence appears in their accounts,' writes Barton, 'showing the persistence of the concept of the "noble savage" even in the face of disagreeable realities.' Several of the writers in this volume, in the middle of harshly realistic descriptions of the weather and the accommodation, switch suddenly and disconcertingly into idealised descriptions of peasant households, which seem to owe nothing to observation and everything to English pastoral poetry.

There were many other reasons for travelling to Lapland; they were summarised energetically by Clarke (who probably originated the term 'literary traveller'):

> What then are the objects, it may be asked, which would induce any literary traveller to venture upon a journey into *Lapland*? Many! That of beholding the face of Nature undisguised; of traversing a strange and almost untrodden territory; of pursuing inquiries which relate to the connexion and the origin of nations; of viewing man as he existed in a primæval state; of gratifying a taste for *Natural History*, by sight of rare *animals, plants*, and *minerals*; of contemplating the various phænomena caused by difference of *climate* and *latitude:* and, to sum up all, the delight which travelling itself affords, independently of any definite object; these are the inducements to such a journey.

Clarke's scientific interests were shared by many other travellers, and are reflected in their frequent references to

Linnaeus and Tycho Brahe. The upper-class Englishmen were, naturally, interested in shooting game and catching salmon, but many other interests, often unexpected, developed during their travels.

Almost all the British travellers attended 'divine service', as they invariably termed it, whenever they could, just as they would back home; it seems not to have concerned them at all that they did not understand a word. Towards the end of the period we find missionaries travelling to Finland with Bibles. It is possible that George Borrow was one of them, but if he was there is no record of the journey which he was contemplating in 1834. Robert Pinkerton left an account of his work in Finland for the British and Foreign Bible Society, while the fullest description is by the 'freelance' missionary John Paterson.

For visitors to Finnish Lapland the route was usually through Sweden, heading for Tornio, but the return journey was often via Ostrobothnia; only later in the nineteenth century did Norway sometimes become a starting point for Lapland. It was very unusual to combine a journey to Lapland with one to southern Finland. All the significant towns, from Tornio to Hamina, were coastal; with the exception of Kaajani there were no chartered towns in central Finland until after quite late in the eighteenth century, so the few travellers who did stray from the coastal routes were in unknown country. Most of those who visited southern Finland were passing through on the way to or from St Petersburg. The road through southern Finland, the Great Coastal Road, was one of three routes; the others were overland through the Baltic states, and the sea-passage straight up the Baltic to Kronstadt (considered by survivors as by far the most dangerous).

The passage between Stockholm and Turku, through the

Åland archipelago, is better documented than the route from Turku to St Petersburg, partly because it usually took longer; travellers on the second stage were never becalmed, or halted by dangerous ice. This journey across the Gulf of Bothnia often left the stronger impression, because of the idyllic scenery in summer or the dramatic dangers of crossing the ice in winter. There were two routes: the packet boats sailed between Stockholm and Turku, while the post route left Grisslehamn for the little village of 'Elsing' (now, confusingly, called Helsinki) about forty miles north of Turku, and usually a two-day journey. Nowadays the 'local' ferry route towards Grisslehamn sails from nearby Kustavi.

The packet boat was more direct, but became increasingly unreliable as winter set in; even in summer it made the traveller largely dependent upon the wind. The 'post route' was a species of island-hopping, with boats available just as horses were always ready at post houses. Although not so dependent on the wind, these travellers could find themselves at the mercy of the elements, and also of unscrupulous postmasters.

The Great Coastal Road, called also 'the great road' or 'The Vyborg Road', is better known now as The King's Road, although that name was not used by British writers. It 'was also known as the Summer Road since it was difficult to traverse in the spring and autumn because of water and broken or weak ice'. The King's Road had been the postal route from Turku to Vyborg since 1638, with post offices added along the route over the years at Karjaa, Helsinki, Porvoo, Loviisa, and Hamina. 'Between the post offices, peasant farmhouses were selected to be postal houses. The ideal situation was for postal houses to be 12–20 kilometres apart', this being the right distance for changing horses. This was the route taken by nearly all the travellers at least until the 1830s. There were two 'ancillary routes', one via Hämeen-linna perhaps taken in part by Pinkerton, and another from Porkkala to Tallinn, which is not mentioned by any British travellers, although it would probably have got them to St Petersburg more quickly. It is worth mentioning here that no traveller from this era mentions using a map, or even comments on not having one.

In the descriptions of those taking this route there is much that is repetitive. After brief impressions of Turku, cursory remarks on the university, the cathedral and the observatory, travellers set off posting towards St Petersburg by way of Salo, Helsinki (with a tour of the fortress at Suomenlinna) and Loviisa. Usually it was their intention to get this part of the journey over as quickly as possible; Elliott, for example, covered the distance from Helsinki to Hamina in one day. For many travellers the limit of their interest was to comment on the carriages in summer or the sledges in winter, on the reliability of the posting system and horses, on the state of the roads and on the condition of the inns, but some of them did linger – not always by choice – and looked beyond their carriages.

Marshall, the earliest recorded traveller, crossed Finland on horseback, but almost all his successors either took their own carriage with them or acquired one en route. Carr paid ten guineas for his chariot to be taken from Harwich, while Clarke bought in Stockholm a huge, luxurious Viennese carriage – 'a monstrous porcupine' – for eighty pounds. Others bought in Turku or St Petersburg a calèche (a four-wheeled carriage sometimes known as a barouche), which usually fell apart before reaching the end of its journey, was bought for a song by the inn landlord when it finally limped to its destination, and was patched up by him to be sold on to the next unsuspecting traveller. In winter most travellers used horse-drawn sledges, which they found faster, safer, and more comfortable than carriages. Coxe's description of his sledge makes it sound quite luxurious.

There was no general agreement about the roads. Their condition was so dependent on the weather, and changed so much from one season to another, that almost every journey was a special case. Pinkerton found them 'almost as good as our English roads, quite level, and covered with gravel and sand', while George Jones wrote that even on the Great Coastal Road near Helsinki 'there does not appear to have been any attempt to form a road, except by cutting down trees, leaving sufficient space for carts and cattle to pass'. For Carr, one of the few redeeming features of travelling in Finland was 'the exposition of every diverging road carefully, and intelligibly, marked out by a directing post'. Every traveller was agreed in praising the efficiency and cheapness of the posting system; it was very rare for horses not to be available. The inns were another matter entirely, and every traveller tells his own tale; it is usually a sad one.

We learn disappointingly little about either the accommodation or the sustenance which travellers experienced in Finland, and much of that little consists of horror stories about the bug-infested hovels which passed as post-houses and wayside inns, with their offerings of rancid fish, sour curds, and bread baked once a year. Coxe was almost a lone voice in praising the grouse: 'we seldom sat down to dinner, even at the commonest inns without being regaled with a brace of those delicious birds'. With only a few exceptions Finland was a route rather than a destination. Wraxall recorded that, in 1774, there were no inns at all between Turku and Helsinki; Clarke elaborated on his complaint:

What is to become of a traveller in the night, in such a country and climate, where there are not only no inns, but where he will find it actually impossible to procure a place of rest; not even a stable, in which he may find clean straw for his couch, or a place where he may lie down?

The answer, for Clarke and for many of his contemporaries, was simple: the 'travelling-carriage was . . . for us our moveable home'. 'Of course,' wrote Wraxall of his journey west from Turku, 'I dined and slept in the carriage, breakfasting each morning at the post-house.' Even when inns were available travellers still preferred to sleep in their own carriage, with the curtains drawn, not unlike modern tourists with their caravan or camper van.

Many of the stops were involuntary – waiting for a wind in Turku, or delayed by a broken carriage. Compared with travellers to Norway at this time, the British made very little contact with the local population. In Norway 'private hospitality was a precondition for travel', with the isolated residential farms of the clergy the commonest resort, while in Sweden travellers were 'well-pleased' with the accommodation offered in country seats. Except in Turku, Helsinki and Hamina, few travellers had any contact with the local residents, or sought any. Opportunities to stay with Finnish families were rare, and even when invitations were given they might not be taken up. Elliott is perhaps typical in this regard: on the packet from Stockholm to Turku he met a professor from Helsinki University who gave him 'letters to a count and countess, both Fins, whose houses are on the road through Finland', but he appears not to have taken up these introductions, and such domestic visits as he did pay were valued chiefly as an opportunity for gathering travel information, to get him on his way as soon as possible. The local gentry were understandably anxious to meet and entertain cultured foreign visitors, but were perhaps more interested in hearing European news than in talking about Finland.

Travellers in northern Finland and Lapland rarely record staying at inns, and were much more likely to stay with the clergy, with wealthy landowners, or at farms. Clarke recorded that in Oulu Baron Silferhielm 'desired that we use his house as his own, while we staid'. Those who journeyed to Lapland went specifically in order to see and experience Lapland; they were not on the way to anywhere else. Certainly, in comparison the the rest of northern Europe, travellers in Lapland experienced a very wide variety of accommodation.

Nearly all these travellers went with an entourage of some sort, but they write very little about their servants, just as, in fashionable novels of the time there is little mention of the domestics. Clarke, for example, staying at the minister's house in Ylitornio, mentions only incidentally 'sending the servants away, to sleep in the village'. A guide was an absolute necessity for the Åland archipelago, and advisable for any deviation from the Great Coastal Road. In continental Europe educated Englishmen could generally get by in French, but in the north an interpreter was essential. A few travellers muddled along with Swedish – Captain Frankland claimed to have managed by talking 'broken English' to Swedes – but none could cope with Finnish, Sami ('Lappish') or Russian. Several travellers took their Swedish interpreter across to Finland, where (except in the occasional Finnish-speaking village) he could be useful until they passed Loviisa, when he was sent back. However ignorant travellers were in the native languages, their education had given most of them Latin, and it is surprising how often this enabled them to communicate, most usefully at the university in

Turku, but also in many parsonages, and even with officials at border crossings. They often commented – as the English still do – on the strange 'foreign' pronunciation of Latin.

During the years covered in this volume Finland became well documented in England. Travel writing was an immensely popular genre – second only to biography and far more prolific than fiction – and Finland had a share of the production. This is confirmed by a writer in the *Monthly Magazine* in July 1827:

> That we have had enough and to spare of travels and voyages in all possible shapes, is, generally speaking, undeniable; and it is but fair to admit that Sweden and the adjacent countries have, within the last twenty years, had their due allotment of descriptive quartos and octavos.

Most of the books presented in this volume went through several editions, nearly all of them were reprinted in America, and some were included in multi-volume collections of travels, for example those edited by Mavor and by Pinkerton. The quarterly and monthly reviews and magazines devoted a lot of space to travel books, and gave very generous excerpts, so even readers who did not actually buy the books could easily learn about them. Finally there was a good deal of travel literature in translation, which further extended knowledge of Finland in England; Acerbi's *Travels through Sweden, Finland, and Lapland* (1802) was the best known of these works, and gained a certain notoriety for an engraving of a sauna scene, the *Edinburgh Review* commenting that 'the Finlandish bath has nothing to recommend it, but the naked accuracy of the representation'.

Like all travel books, these works tell us, often unintentionally, a good deal about the men who wrote them. (It is not until the late 1820s that a British woman made a record-ed journey to Finland.) The English abroad have a certain reputation for behaving uncompromisingly and even eccentrically, and for refusing to adapt to unfamiliar conditions. There were few travellers to Finland who did not, to some degree, take their prejudices abroad with them; Elliott was well aware of this tendency to chauvinism:

> You have no doubt observed, as I have, that the English are universally respected, feared and envied in foreign countries, but never loved. Our countrymen are too conscious of their superiority as a nation, and frequently too little conscious of their inferiority as individuals. Instead of wishing to learn what they may from other nations, and to acquaint themselves with the opinions of foreigners on subjects of moral, political and scientific interest, they either strive to impose on them their habits and views, or else conduct themselves with a degree of reserve which is construed into hauteur.

To what extent this judgement is true modern readers may now decide for themselves.

Joseph Marshall

So little is known about Joseph Marshall that his very existence has been called into doubt. Although there is no biographical information about him, his personality and interests come over very strongly in his writing. The range of these interests is indicated in the full title of his book, published in 1772: *Travels through Holland, Flanders, Germany, Denmark, Sweden, Lapland, Russia, The Ukraine and Poland in the Years 1768, 1769, and 1770. In which is particularly Minuted The Present State of Those Countries respecting their Agriculture, Population, Manufactures, Commerce, the Arts, and Useful Undertakings.*

In his Preface Marshall writes confessionally about his disappointment with the Grand Tour which he had undertaken some eleven years earlier, and which had seen him 'running very eagerly after every thing produced by the fine arts, and thinking that painting, statuary, music, and the like, were the only objects worthy of notice'. His considered verdict was that he had learned nothing, and that his life had not been improved. So when a melancholy mood produced by 'a family loss' led him to 'seek for that amusement in travelling, which my own country I found would not afford', he had no wish to revisit France or Italy:

> I determined to spend some years in journeying through the Northern Parts, which would probably present me with a new world; the accounts I had read of most of them, being either very imperfect, or so old, that every thing might be altered since the authors wrote, so that I ran no risque of knowing too much before I set out.

Marshall reminds me frequently of his contemporary, the agriculturalist Arthur Young, as well as of William Cobbett on his *Rural Rides* through nineteenth-century England. At every point he is sizing up the economic realities, comparing what he sees to his own practice as a farmer, looking at the system of land-management, and lamenting the lost opportunities which he sees around him. He did not, for instance, favour Finnish peasants owning their own land, since this led to them growing only enough for their own use. If they had to pay rent to an enterprising landlord, the economic potential of the land would, Marshall felt, be realised.

Marshall's route through Finland was an unusual one, and was not followed by any of the other travellers of this era. He entered the country from Sweden at Tornio, on his Dalecarlian horse, whose hardiness and reliability he praised unstintingly. He left on 31 July 1768, and followed the coast to 'Coyrannum' (presumably Kuivaniemi), 'a little town on the coast'. He found the natives not 'so intelligent or comprehensive' as further south:

> but they are a very simple and harmless people, and appear to be very humane. I found most of them exceedingly respectful and civil. Their ordinary salutation is not bowing, like the Swedes in other parts: these countrymen take hold of your right-hand, and lay it over their left, making strange faces at the same time.

His route south is not easy to trace; after two days and eighty miles he arrived at 'Salo' (presumably Saloinen, just south of Raahe) 'the next town, of the least consequence'. Since he does not mention Oulu or Raahe, he must have gone inland: 'the country through which I travelled not mountainous, being in general a plain, rising into small hills'.

A few days later, after 'twice taking up my lodging with

very hospitable farmers', one of whose 'crops were all very fine and clean', he arrived at Uusikaarlepyy, 'a place of no great consideration'. He concedes that 'it is not . . . badly built, and the streets are regular. The church is small but very neat'. He travelled on to Vaasa, which he calls 'Wassay'. There the landlord of his inn told him that

> in the next room were a set of gentlemen of the town, assembled at a club, who, understanding that there was a stranger in the house, sent their compliments to him, inviting him to spend the evening with them.

The principal member of the 'club' was a corpulent former merchant captain, who spoke French and was able to act as interpreter. Known as the Captain, he was widely travelled, and was regarded as an 'oracle' by those present. They appeared to be 'people of substance', 'all decently and neatly dressed', but what most struck Marshall was their heavy smoking and drinking:

> The worst of their company was their pipes; they all smoaked tobacco incessantly; and as the room was but a small one, I thought that I should have been suffocated at first. They made many inquiries after England, and our manners and customs in many particulars; in which I satisfied them, much to their apparent entertainment. I, in my turn, questioned them about the manufactures and commerce of their town and neighbourhood, and they gave me an account of every thing they could, and I believe a very just one.

He was invited to join them for supper, which 'relieved me for a time from the effluvia of their pipes'. He discovered that he 'gained much in all their good graces, by thinking their country worth viewing thro' curiosity', but found that did he not long remain the the main object of their interest when several of the party 'seemed to pay their addresses to a bottle of brandy'.

> After supper they all took to their pipes again, to my no small mortification; and pushing about the bottle again pretty briskly, they were not long altogether so clear-headed as I could have wished for, in order to have gained some more intelligence.

The following day he was invited to a dinner with the Captain:

> I accepted his invitation, and went accordingly, and found a company of six or seven, among whom was a clergyman, an elderly man, of an agreeable aspect; as he did not understand French, I was some time with but little conversation with him; but he asking me if I spoke Latin, I was taken by surprize, and after a little confusion, recollected myself enough to carry on a tolerable conversation with him afterwards, and found him a sensible, modest man.

One of this group, Mr Hirzel, had a small estate 'on the north point of the Holla lake', 120 miles inland, and invited Marshall to visit it with him; the description makes it clear that this was Lake Päijänne. He was persuaded to head for his destination, St Petersburg, via Vyborg, which was recommended to him as 'a very short cut' compared with his intended route via Turku. He gives a vivid account of his journey to this estate, revealing again and again his curiosity and concern for the practical and economic aspects of the land. He was also deeply impressed by the beauty of the landscape:

> The country here is very fine. The lake is a noble one, of a varying breadth, from three to more than twenty

miles over; and the length is above an hundred; there are numerous islands in it, some of them two or three miles broad, and many others less. At the northern point of it, is one of these islands, about two miles from the main land, which is a part of Mr. Hirzel's possession. We came down to a few cottages on the shore, which he has built, and where a sloop lies always in readiness to carry him over; into this we got, leaving our horses in a barn by the cottage, and taking all our baggage with us in the vessel. In crossing the water, I was much delighted with the views; the hills in some places rise very boldly from the lake, which has a beautiful effect, as the whole country is covered with thick woods. The island is four miles long, and three broad, consisting of various land, but in general high and dry, and most of it a wood: Mr. Hirzel built a small house here, of four rooms on a floor, having two tolerable parlours, and the whole neatly furnished: in it we found a servant and his family, who has the management of a small farm: near it are barns, stables, and other offices; and four cottages, which he also built, and are inhabited by peasants; to each of whom he assigned a small farm, which he obliges them to cultivate very neatly. It is highly necessary that they should be good farmers; for the subsistence of themselves and cattle much depends on it, being at such a distance from any other habitation. Mr. Hirzel directs his own manager so, as to oblige him always to have a good store of all products before hand. He has a cellar well filled, plenty of fish and game at command; and his farm yields him all common provisions, with good fowls: so that he is always sure of finding good eating and drinking: he has a large boat-house, under which his sloop can run; and several open boats. After

dinner we took a walk about his farm, which seemed to
be very well managed, and the crops good; at which I
do not wonder; for the soil of the island is a fine black,
dry, deep mold, peculiarly adapted, I should suppose,
for all husbandry applications. As I had expressed a
desire of sailing a little on the lake, for the pleasure of
viewing the woods, Mr. Hirzel manned the sloop, in the
morning of the 12th; and having laid in a stock of provisions and my bed, said, he would make a three days
voyage for my entertainment; he steered south by the
east shore, and returned by the west: we made many
leagues, having a favourable wind, gaining very near
the south end of the lake: nothing could be more agreeable; the water beautiful, and the surrounding country extremely various. We lived well; for his nets and
hooks were excellently managed, and supplied us with
many sorts of fine fish in great perfection, which we
dressed and eat with an admirable stomach. We caught
one carp that weighed sixteen pounds, and Mr. Hirzel
told me that he has taken them of a larger size; but they
are not so well tasted as those of about six or seven
pounds. Here are also pike, and tench, but not equal to
what I have eat elsewhere; eels exceeding good; and a
fish about the size of a trout, and of the same shape, but
much superior flavour, which they call a *snout*. – I must
confess that this was one of the most agreeable voyages
I had ever made. We had about half a day in which the
wind being brisk, the waves ran pretty high, and gave
us the exercise of beating over them.

The 15th, Mr. Hirzel dedicated to shooting, for which
sport we did not go off the island; he had a leash of
spaniels there that found us plenty of game; these were
pheasants and hares, with a few partridges; but none

of them equal in taste to the same sorts in England; we had a very good day's work to range about only a part of the island; and, having killed game enough for our use and amusement, returned home.

Marshall was overwhelmed by the thought of the economic potential of this land, if the produce could only be got to market, and he records in enthusiastic detail Mr Hirzel's plans for opening up the river to the Gulf of Bothnia. After some days he continued on his way, and thus became – by a period of many years – the first English traveller to provide any account of the Finnish lakelands. His description of this second leg of his journey, via Pieksamäki ('Pexama') to Savonlinna is disappointingly brief, so is worth giving in full:

From this island of my friend Mr. Hirzel, I was determined what route I should take to Petersburg: upon consideration, and after making many enquiries I resolved to go through the province of Savolax to the capital of it, the only town of any note in it, which is Nyslot; and thence to Wyburg in my way to the Russian capital. The 17th, in the morning I took my leave of Mr. Hirzel and his friend, and set off for Pexama, a little town at the distance of seventy miles; which is all through the forest: it took me two days; but I met with no houses; therefore all my refreshment and rest was a meal taken on the grass, and a nap upon the same pillow. I have seen a Swedish map, which places seven villages in the road; but I had now sufficient reason to pronounce it erroneous: the country is all a rich soil, and covered in most places very thickly with fine timber: A country, which would feed numerous inhabitants; and is all admirably watered; for I was more than once in sight of great lakes; but it is in the most desolate condition, and yields not any advantage to its possessors. From Pexama to Nyslot is between fifty and sixty miles; all the way on the banks of a very noble lake, which, from its narrowness and winding course, has exactly the appearance of a great river. The country is all forest; but I saw two or three villages; at one of which I took up my lodging: there were some small farms, which appeared to be tolerably cultivated; and I found that this lake, along which I had passed, was navigable quite to the gulph of Finland; and that the villages I saw were owing to this circumstance; for the timber of the forest was convey'd thither to advantage; and the cutting and preparing it found employment for the people.

He concludes the Finnish part of his account with a description of Savonlinna:

Nyslot is a neat little town beautifully situated in a nook of land, that runs into the lake, with which it is chiefly surrounded. The church is a new building and handsome; the streets are some of them well paved and tolerably built; and there was an appearance of wealth among the inhabitants, all of which I found was owing to the timber trade: for two or three miles round the town the country is well cultivated, and shows plainly what the rest is capable of, did it possess the same advantages of a market.

Marshall was a pioneer; his is the first published account of Finland in English. He was an Enlightenment traveller, writes Barton, who 'looked at nature in terms of the natural resources it provided to meet human needs'. Vigorous and practical, with his distinctively plain vocabulary and clunky syntax, he left the appreciation of the finer cultural aspects of Finland to those who came after him.

Sir Nathaniel William Wraxall

The next British traveller to have published his travels, Nathaniel Wraxall, moved in very different circles from Marshall. The son of a Bristol merchant, he went, before he was twenty, to work for the East India Company in Bombay, where he prospered for two years, serving as Judge-Advocate and Paymaster. After returning to Europe he travelled extensively, especially in Portugal and in Northern Europe. On his travels he met several Danish noblemen who had been exiled for their support of the deposed Queen Caroline Matilda, sister of George III. She died before Wraxall's attempts to persuade George III to act on her behalf had got anywhere. From 1780 to 1794 he was a Member of Parliament, and after resigning he devoted his time mainly to writing, becoming one of the earliest professional travel writers in English. He was created a baronet in 1813.

He travelled to St Petersburg during the spring and summer of 1774, and published his *Cursory Remarks made in a Tour through some of the Northern Parts of Europe, particularly Copenhagen, Stockholm and Petersburg* in 1775. The elegance of his writing contrasts noticeably with the immediacy and abruptness of Marshall's, but the phrase 'cursory remarks' reveals another difference: he was, at least at this time, more a dilettante than a serious traveller or explorer. Aware of this, perhaps, he omitted the phrase from the title in the subsequent editions.

William Mavor thought highly enough of Wraxall to include his book in a series entitled *Historical Account of the most Celebrated Voyages, Travels, and Discoveries* in 1797, introducing Wraxall as one who was already a celebrity:

> The ingenious author of this tour is so well known, that it is unnecessary, in the present day, to give any particulars respecting him; and posterity will be at no loss to distinguish him among those who have contributed to inform or amuse the public, by his various valuable publications.

In his praise of Wraxall's achievements Mavor sets out quite explicitly the qualities expected in a travel book at this time, qualities which several contemporary chroniclers of Finland signally failed to possess:

> Mr. Wraxall's object on this occasion, was to visit the three northern capitals and courts, and to describe the prominent features of each. He has not, however, been inattentive to other subjects which solicit the regard of an enlightened traveller. He has neither encumbered his narrative with details, which more properly belong to history and geography; nor omitted such a view of the scenes through which he passed, as was likely to afford entertainment and instruction.

Andrew Swinton offered much fainter praise in the Preface to his own *Travels* (1792):

> It is impossible to disregard either the admirable alacrity of this Gentleman's movements, or to suppose that he had it in his power to draw many of his reflections from actual observation.

Wraxall, perhaps encouraged by Mavor's compliments, revised his book, and published it in a fourth edition as *A Tour round the Baltic* in 1807. This new edition shows a great deal of stylistic polishing, and a softening of many of his harsher opinions. It also contains a lot more detail about Finland, presumably taken from the journal he kept at the time.

Wraxall's interests and viewpoint are, like his style, very different from Marshall's. He displays little curiosity about the country, and very limited enthusiasm for what he sees. Although he travelled in idyllic June weather, the very existence of the northern winters still disgusted him. He had already expressed his opinions in a letter from Sweden:

> So great is my detestation of these inhospitable and polar countries, that no honours or fortunes could tempt me to remain in them, and I would rather reside in a cottage beneath a temperate and genial heaven than in a palace invested so many months with ice and darkness.

Even such places, though, had their contribution to make to a serious traveller's total experience:

> Some parts of the globe are, however, infinitely more exuberant and rich in the materials for producing elegant delight than others. In some they are so wantonly and plenteously scattered, that stupidity itself must catch some portion of their power of pleasing. In others they lie deeper beneath the surface, and like unpolished gems only glitter in the eye of clear and perspicuous observation. – Such are the kingdoms which I am about to visit, covered during many months with snow, and wrapt in all the horrors of a polar winter: unpolished in their manners, and still retaining the vestiges of Gothic ignorance, they present not many charms to tempt the traveller. The Roman arms never penetrated into these inhospitable climes, nor is the Antiquarian allured to pass their snows by the venerable remains of amphitheatres, temples, and naumachiæ. Yet even in

these remote and inclement kingdoms, are the seeds of knowledge scattered; and if the mind receives no pleasure from the reflection of their past greatness or refinement, yet may it be enlarged and improved from the consideration of their present comparative power and importance in the scale of Europe.

Wraxall took the Great Coastal Road, travelling from Stockholm via Turku to St Petersburg; his is the first published account of this route in English. The boat journey through the Åland archipelago was what he liked best, but even here he was reluctant to appreciate the scenery for what it was, and preferred to single out aspects of the picturesque, or to imagine himself among the islands of classical Greece. He engaged a boat at Grisslehamn, in 'remarkably serene and pleasant' weather, and 'ordered my carriage . . . to be put into the boat, and following it myself we set sail'. He landed on Eckerö, where he breakfasted at 'a very tolerable inn', before crossing the island, and taking a boat over the 'narrow channel' to Åland. Here he was greeted by the governor, and took 'the opportunity of gaining a little information relative to the island'. The only experience in all of Finland which he recorded with any enthusiasm was on the island of Sund; he visited the dangerously ruined Kastelholm, where he clambered on hands and knees through piles of fallen masonry to the trap-door into the dungeon where King Erik XIV had been incarcerated:

> I must own I was struck with compassion and horror, at reflecting that a sovereign had been the tenant of such a dungeon, which is too miserable for the worst malefactor . . . The flooring is of brick, and, as the peasant pretended to show me, is worn away in those places where the king was used to walk . . .

I left Castleholm after I had gratified my curiosity, and continuing my journey, arrived at the termination of the island, as the sun set. It was my intention to have gone on to Finland by the post rout, through several small islands or rocks, from one to another, of which there are constantly boats provided to convey travellers. Just as I was on the point of carrying this design into execution, four or five of the country people came and proposed to convey me from thence straight to Abo. They said, the distance was only about one hundred and twenty English miles, that the wind was very fair; that they had often made the passage in twelve or fourteen hours, and doubted not to do the same now; finally, that I needed not lose a moment, as their little vessel was in readiness, and only waited my orders. I did not hesitate long, but complied with the offer, and left Aland about midnight on Saturday.

I slept, as I had done the preceding night, in my carriage, and at seven the ensuing morning found myself in a narrow passage, surrounded by high rocks, and the people employed in rowing. I made no question that we were already in the river of Abo, but was not a little chagrined to find on enquiry, that the wind had fallen away, that we were hardly thirty miles from the place we had quitted, and that I must not flatter myself with landing in Finland that day. They added, that the whole way was thro' such channels as I was then in; that some of the islands by which I sailed were inhabited; and that if I pleased, they would land me on one of them, where I might procure some refreshment. To this proposition I gladly consented, and about nine o'clock I went ashore on one called Lappo. I walked to a little hamlet at a mile distance from the shore: the poor peasants very chearfully brought me some cream, and assisted in boiling my coffee. Nothing could exceed their poverty; a little black bread, fish, pork, and a sort of mixture they called beer, constituting all their sustenance.

After having made a very comfortable breakfast on this unknown and sequestered island, I returned again to the boat. During the whole day, we pursued our voyage through a labyrinth of small rocks and isles, many of them covered with firs and aspins; some few green and beautiful, but far the greater number barren and rugged. I could have fancied myself among the Cyclades, so famous in ancient story; but here were no temples sacred to Apollo or to Juno; nor had genius and poetry conspired to render every cliff and promontory immortal. Many of the prospects were, however, wondrously picturesque and romantic, and I frequently stopped the boatmen for a minute, to gaze upon the extraordinary scene around me. Sometimes we went through channels of only twenty or thirty feet in breadth; sometimes the water opened into a considerable expanse; and often there appeared to be no avenue on any side. I was astonished how they so exactly knew their track, in this intricate and perplexing maze, through which nothing besides long experience could have conducted them. We were about forty miles from Abo when the sun went down, and I was once more obliged to sleep in my carriage: we entered the river early yesterday morning, and about eight o'clock I finished my voyage.

For a fashionable young man in search of the picturesque the town of Turku had nothing at all to offer:

There is not any thing [*1807 reads 'very little'*] in Abo, which has entertained me in the survey, or can amuse

36

you by the description. It is a wretched capital of a barbarous province. The houses are almost all of wood,
and the archiepiscopal palace is composed of no better materials, except that it is painted red. I enquired
if there was not any object in the university to merit
attention; but they assure me that it would be regarded as a piece of ridicule, to visit it on such an errand,
there being nothing within it's walls except a very small
library, and a few philosophical instruments.

In Uppsala Wraxall had found consolation for his disap-
pointments in a visit from Linnaeus; in Turku a hot afternoon was rendered tolerable only by concentrating his view
on scenes which were – at least potentially – picturesque:

There is at this time a great annual fair, and I have
amused myself this hour past, in looking from the window of my apartment, at a crowd of three or four thousand Finland peasants, who are collected together, and
form a curious *coup d'œil* in their country dresses.

Wraxall visited the castle, 'now in ruins; . . . the chapel
only remains entire, and is still appropriated to divine worship'. There was only one other piece of sightseeing, which
clearly did not excite him: 'From the tower of the cathedral
of Abo, I had an extensive view of the country, which is flat
on every side'.

His journey to Helsinki reveals a good deal about the difficulties of travelling in Finland at this time, even on the
Great Coastal Route:

I was near forty-eight hours in driving from Abo to
Helsingfors, during which time I never stopped, except to change horses. Inns there were, indeed, none
between the two places. Of course, I dined and slept

in the carriage, breakfasting each morning at the post-house. I have not experienced more intense heat even in Portugal, than I have found in the sixty-second degree of northern latitude; the sun scarcely disappearing at this season, for more than three hours; and the light being such at midnight, as to allow me to write, or to distinguish objects accurately, at several miles distance. In various places I passed through woods which were in flames, as the peasants are accustomed to set fire to the firs, in order to fructify the soil with the ashes. I could have fancied myself among the wilds of America. Yet, Finland is not so unfertile or uncultivated a province, as I had been taught to expect. I saw no part of Sweden, except East Gothland, which is so free from those vast stones, that nature in her anger scattered over these kingdoms; nor any, where the soil is apparently more fertile, or the country better peopled. The peasants speak a barbarous jargon, equally unintelligible to a Swede or a Russian; but, in the towns, the former language is generally used, and generally understood.

Wraxall stayed a day in Helsinki, 'more to recover my past fatigue, than from the desire of seeing an immense fortress built as a barrier against the Russians'. This is the first of many references during this period to Suomenlinna, (in Swedish Sveaborg), constructed between 1748 and 1788. It was Finland's greatest – indeed its only – tourist attraction:

It is not yet entirely completed; but as more than two thirds of the soldiery are constantly at work on the fortifications, it is to be presumed that it will be in full readiness for the next rupture between these rival nations.

'Tho' it blew very fresh,' he records, 'I went off to it in a boat.' He was permitted 'to visit the works, accompanied by an officer'. 'As far as art can render it impregnable,' he concluded, 'no efforts seem to have been omitted.'

Quitting Helsingfors, I continued my journey towards Borgo, capital of the province of Nyland. The road lay frequently through deep woods, abounding in wild strawberries, which the peasants brought me. It was about a quarter past ten o'clock, on the evening of the 24th of June, when I entered Borgo, the sun then shining bright above the horizon. Borgo is a tolerable town, pleasingly situated on a hill, at the foot of which runs a small river. The university, or as they more modestly denominate it, the Gymnasium, is built of stone. I visited this seat of letters, which contains only about sixty students, and seven professors, within its walls. In the hall, or convocation-chamber, I found the professors all assembled, and one of them had the goodness to conduct me over the building. It was constructed by the late king Adolphus, the former Gymnasium having been completely demolished by the Russians: a fate that has likewise more than once attended the town of Borgo; its situation, near the frontiers, exposing it to the ravages of war.

I reached Louisa, in the afternoon of the 25th; a town which was likewise founded, in 1757, by the late king; who, whatever were the defects of his character, as a sovereign of vigor or decision, seems to have extended the most vigilant attention to this vulnerable portion of the Swedish dominions. Louisa was so called after the present queen dowager; like Caieta, in antiquity, after the nurse of Eneas. It is difficult to depicture the aspect of the country in which Louisa stands. For the space of at least a league before I arrived there, and for more than two leagues after I quitted it, the earth may almost be said to have disappeared from my view; so completely was it covered by stones, or rather rocks: for, many of them, from their magnitude, may well merit that appellation. It seems as if they had fallen from the sky; and Ovid, had he been acquainted with this portion of the globe, might here have placed the 'Campi Phlegræi,' where Jupiter overcame the Titans. The road, compelled to respect these formidable impediments, performs a thousand tortuous evolutions, in order to avoid them, and serpentines beautifully for many miles. Neither cultivation, not population, can possibly exist amongst such a wilderness of stones. Yet, Louisa is built in the very centre of this desert; and I not only found there a very tolerable inn; but, was charged no more than four copper dollars, or one shilling English money, for an excellent dinner.

It was nearly midnight, when I arrived at the bank of the river Kymen, which here divides the empire of Russia from the dominions of Sweden. The stream is above two hundred feet broad, and across it is a wooden bridge, one half of which is constantly repaired by the one, and the other half by the other nation. I was stopped by the guards on either side, and underwent a very minute search before I was permitted to proceed. A league beyond this boundary, my carriage broke down in a deep wood, more than two English miles from any cottage: it was about four in the morning when the accident happened; and as the case was urgent, I was compelled to leave the postilion to guard the chaise, while I walked on with my servant, to the next Russian hamlet. We addressed ourselves to the first peasant we met, who was fortunately a Swede by birth, and understood the language. After much entreaty, I prevailed on him to furnish me with a wheel from his own little cart, as my carriage could not have been repaired in many hours, and the people even declared it incurable from it's long services, and numerous ailments. I thought myself very happy to procure this temporary aid, and by the help of it I arrived at Kupis, the first post in Russian Finland.

The mistress of the inn at Kupis, not only set before me strawberries and cream, but persisted in refusing to accept of any compensation for her hospitality. Having refitted the carriage, I proceeded, and began soon to become sensible that I had quitted the dominions of Gustavus, for those of Catherine. At Hogfors, which is distant only about twenty-four miles from the bank of the Kymen, I entered the province of Carelia. Here, the men who surrounded the carriage when I stopped to change horses, could not either speak, or understand, a word of Swedish. The women were differently habited, evidently of another race: and the manners of both sexes were more obsequious than I had found them in Finland, or in Sweden. I reached Fredricshamm about six the same evening, where this national contrast was still more complete. It is the first Russian town and garrison. Here every thing announced a different people from those I had just quitted. The features, the complexion, the dress of the inhabitants were all Muscovite; and a thousand leagues of distance could not have made a more striking alteration. The same remark is exactly true, in crossing the Pyrenees, from French, into Spanish, Navarra; and plainly evinces how strongly the character of the individuals, which compose society, is tinged and formed by the government, policy, and religion of the nation.

This was the only place in Finland in which Wraxall chose to spend a day when he could have travelled on, perhaps because of the 'unaffected politeness and hospitality' which was extended to him by the governor, General Setikoff. His responses to Hamina were mixed:

> The plan of Fredricshamm, is elegant, and realises in miniature that commonly attributed to Sir Christopher Wren, after the fire of London, in 1666, all the streets going off like Radii from a centre, in which is built a handsome Hotel-de-ville. But, the houses are very mean, being composed only of a single floor; and the streets, which are unpaved, have only a loose, deep sand, in which the passenger sinks up to the ankle, at every step.

He described 'the whole intermediate country' between Hamina and Vyborg as 'the most savage, rocky, and inhospitable desert you can conceive, from the gates of one, to the entrance of the other'.

Wraxall's concluding remarks are, perhaps, more thoughtful than any other observation he made about Finland:

> Yet, has this barren frontier of the Swedish and Russian territory been as obstinately disputed, and caused the effusion of as much blood, as the most plentiful or happy regions of the earth.

William Coxe

When William Coxe died in 1828, at the age of eighty, he had spent half of his life as Archdeacon of Wiltshire and a prebendary of Salisbury cathedral. He was a noted antiquarian, and had edited several valuable eighteenth-century memoirs.

His early experiences were very different from this life of ecclesiastical calm and mild academic distinction. As a young man he had been a Fellow of King's College, Cambridge, and became travelling tutor to the son and heir of the Earl of Pembroke and Montgomery, accompanying him on a trip to Russia. This was only the first of Coxe's travels; he went on to make at least four more major European tours, including a return to northern Europe in 1784–5, before he settled down. His *Travels into Poland, Russia, Sweden, and Denmark* (1784) reached a fifth edition in 1802, dedicated to the new Earl, his former travelling companion.

In comparison to Wraxall's florid style, Coxe's writing is rather austere, and shows the influence of Samuel Johnson's recently published *A Journey to the Western Isles of Scotland* (1775). Coxe's *Travels* provided the most widely-read account of Finland during this period. John Pinkerton, who included them in his *A General Collection of the Best and Most Interesting Voyages and Travels in all Parts of the World* (1808-14), commented that 'the high value of this work is well-known, and has been fully appreciated by numerous translations abroad'. Barton considers that 'Coxe set a benchmark for travel literature of the North', and that he was considered an authority by later writers. Swinton gave a less favourable opinion: 'He has given us many accurate and useful details . . . These, together with historical extracts from a great number of Writers . . . swell his volumes to a respectable size as well as price.'

As the title of the book indicates, the travellers followed an anti-clockwise route around the Baltic. They left St Petersburg for Vyborg on February 3, 1779, and Coxe gives a detailed and often entertaining account of winter travelling; his is the first of many travellers' accounts of the perilous crossing of the Åland archipelago in winter. His description of his travelling clothes provides an amusing picture of an Englishman who is going to take no chances with the weather; Coxe seems to have been disappointed that it was never quite cold enough for him to justify wearing the whole lot:

> On the evening of the 3d of February, 1779, we took our departure from Petersburgh, and, travelling all night, arrived on the following day at Wiburgh. I took the following precautions to guard against the cold. I had on a suit of Bath-drugget lined with flannel; two pair of worsted stockings; slippers, over which I drew boots well secured with flannel and fur: these boots I generally wore in the carriage, but pulled off when I entered a house. If the weather had proved uncommonly severe, I was provided with a kind of sheep-skin case, with the wool on the inside for each of my legs, which reached to my waist, and was large enough to enclose my boots. I wrapped round my body a great coat of blue nankeen lined with lamb-skin, and occasionally added a large *pelisse*, or fur robe. I had a bear's-skin muff; and my head was enveloped in a black velvet cap quilted with silk and cotton, which covered my cheeks, was tied under my chin, and might, if necessary, be drawn over the face. Thus accoutred, I could venture

to defy even the cold of Lapland, whither our course was directed.

Our train consisted of eight sledges, including those appropriated to the baggage, as, on account of the narrowness of the roads, each person had a separate carriage. There are various kinds of sledges used in this country: some are entirely close; others quite open; those which we employed were partly open, and partly covered. A sledge of this sort is shaped like a cradle; its tilt, which rises from the hinder extremity, and projects to about two feet, was open in front, but provided with curtains, which might be drawn and tied together whenever the weather was severe. The outside was secured with matting and oil-skin; and the inside with coarse cloth. Within was a mattrass, feather-bed and coverlid, or quilt of coarse cloth. In this travelling coach I sometimes lay extended at full length; sometimes sat cross-legged like a Turk; and at other times raised myself on a seat formed by two cushions. Each sledge was drawn by two horses, which, on account of the narrowness of the roads, were harnessed one before the other. The usual rate of travelling is from six to eight miles in the hour. The motion of the carriage over the beaten snow was so easy as to be almost imperceptible; and I never performed any journey in a more commodious manner.

Though we continued our route during the night, and there was no moon; yet an *Aurora Borealis* and the whiteness of the snow, supplied an agreeable species of twilight. The road, or rather path, through which our route lay, was scarcely more than a yard in breadth, sunk two or three feet beneath the level of the snow, and hardened by the repeated pressure of horses and sledges. When two carriages met in this narrow track, the horses, which turned out of the way, sunk into the soft untrodden snow as high as their girths.

Coxe enjoyed his first impressions of Finland as his sledge sped towards Hamina; few other travellers of the era found such attractions in the landscape of Eastern Finland, or such pleasure in travelling this part of the Great Coastal Road:

> There was no moon, or even the smallest gleam of an *Aurora Borealis,* yet the snow cast a strong light; and our train of sledges made a very picturesque appearance as they winded round the whitened hills, pierced into the thick forests, or extended in a straight line along the frozen surface of the lakes. During our course, the still silence of the night was relieved by the carols of our drivers, who frequently sang the most simple and pleasing airs. In this progress I beguiled the length of the journey, either by listening to their songs echoed by the surrounding forests, by admiring the unusual cast of the nocturnal scenery, or by slumbering in my travelling couch as comfortably as in a bed . . .
>
> Feb. 6. We arrived about nine in the morning at Fredricksham, and took up our lodging at an inn, where we met with very comfortable accommodations.

Here they dined with the commander of the garrison:

> Our host, an old German officer, who had seen much service, and possessed all that liberal frankness generally conspicuous in veterans, enlivened an excellent entertainment with the vivacity of his conversation. The floors of the apartments, instead of being covered with carpets, were, according to a custom not unusual in these parts, strewed with leaves and small twigs of

pines and firs, which afford, when bruised, a pleasant smell, and give a cleanly appearance to the rooms.

Coxe was the first of many writers to describe the pleasant contrast when entering Finland from Russia. For about two hundred years this was the usual response of those who crossed the Russian border, although there were a few striking dissidents:

> The peasants of Finland differ materially from the Russians in their look and dress: they had for the most part fair complexions, and many of them red hair; they shave their beards, wear their hair parted at the top, and hanging to a considerable length over their shoulders. We could not avoid remarking, that they were in general more civilized than the Russians; and that even in the smallest villages we were able to procure much better accommodations, than we usually met with in the largest towns which we had hitherto visited in this empire.

As they crossed the Kymijoki into 'Swedish Finland' they experienced the 'ceremony' of having their baggage 'slightly searched' by the custom-house officers at each end of the the bridge. In Loviisa Coxe thought that the red-painted houses looked 'much neater than those of the common towns and villages in Russia'. The governor, 'a sensible well-informed old man, of Scotch extraction, who had served during several years in France, in the Royal Swedish regiment', tried to encourage him to see more of the country:

> 'You have probably conceived a bad opinion of Finland, from the regions which you have already traversed, which are the most desolate part of the province; but I assure you, that a few miles from the sea-coast it is a

very agreeable country, fertile in pasture, rye, oats, and barley.'

It is a great pity that so much 'very agreeable country' remained undiscovered by a generation of travellers like Wraxall and Coxe, who were in too much of a hurry to stop, or even to look around to any extent. It is unfortunate, too, that it was this officer who actually advised him that the passage over the ice from Turku to Stockholm was practicable; despite his strong wish to see Lapland, Coxe was dissuaded from cutting cross-country towards Vaasa to take the land route to Stockholm via Tornio. Without this advice, he might have been been able to give some account of central Finland; instead, like so many others, he followed the southern coastal route.

They set off at eight in the evening, 'lighted during the whole night by a beautiful *Aurora Borealis*', and

arrived on the ensuing morning at Helsingfors, which stands in a romantick situation, upon a rising shore, near several rocks and huge fragments of granite. Within a small distance of Helsingfors and close to the gulf, the Swedes were constructing a fortress which, when finished, will be the strongest in these parts. The harbour is the most commodious in Finland.

The sheer size of Suomenlinna impressed visitors as nothing else in Finland did or could; they could hardly have been more amazed by the pyramids. In the later editions of his book Coxe gives a description of how it appeared when he saw it during his second trip to Finland:

The works are really stupendous and worthy of the ancient Romans. The walls are chiefly of hewn granite, covered with earth, from six to ten feet thick, and in a few places not less than 48 in height. The batteries, which begin upon a level with the water, and rise in tiers one above the other in all directions, commanding the only channel through which large vessels can sail to Helsingfors, render the passage of an enemy's fleet extremely dangerous, if not impracticable.

In Helsinki, at the governor's invitation, they attended a ball, where

the gentlemen and ladies all wore the new Swedish dress; and amused themselves chiefly with minuets and English country dances. The company were very polite and attentive to us, and several accosted us in French.

Two days of travelling 'through a tract of country that seemed better peopled than the other parts of Finland which we had hitherto traversed; and which was diversified with a beautiful mixture of hill and dale' took them to Turku, which Coxe paid little attention to, remarking merely that 'the town . . . is not ill built'. At least, unlike Wraxall, he visited the university, commenting on the 'near 10,000 volumes' in the library. He mentioned briefly the botanical garden, the cathedral, and the castle.

'About forty miles from Abo' – presumably at the little settlement of Helsinki (Elsing) – they arrived at the Gulf of Bothnia, and set out over the ice, stopping the first night on the island of Vartsala, where they 'found a comfortable village' for their night's lodging.

Feb. 14. We sat out early: the weather was hazy and unpromising, and a strong breeze began to freshen. The post was about 18 miles in length: we passed many small islands and rocks; some covered with underwood, and sprinkled with villages; others were nothing but bare granite, without a single habitation or tree. In a few places the ice of the gulf was a smooth sheet; in others it was roughly frozen in waves and large masses. The vast extended plain of ice, broken in abrupt ridges, the boundless and dreary track marked only by a line of trees and boughs, and the rugged rocks starting up on every side, afforded one of the most desolate scenes imaginable.

We changed horses at Brando, an island which contained six or seven villages, a church, some arable land, and small woods. About three we arrived on the island Cumlin, 36 miles from Varisala; and as the next post was above thirty miles, we prudently took up our quarters in a peasant's cottage, rather than again encounter the hazards of a journey by night. The peasants were well clothed; the men wore long cloth coats lined with sheep-skin; the women a striped kind of woollen stuff, of mixed colours, chiefly green, white, and red: they seemed very honest; and our servants had no occasion to employ the same vigilance in watching the luggage as was requisite in Russia. The cottages were built like those in Russia, with whole trees piled one upon the other, and mortaised and tenanted at each extremity; the timbers of several were sawed on the outside in the form of planks. They generally contain two or three apartments, small, but neat and clean; have all brick chimnies, and a semicircular fire-place high and narrow, in which the wood is placed upright, and by means of birch-bark instantaneously kindled. The villagers possessed many conveniences of life, which we did not meet with in Russia, particularly beds, and a greater variety of household furniture.

While our dinner was preparing, we strolled to a

wind-mill situated on an eminence, from whence we commanded a full view of the island, which seemed a huge pile of rocks of red and grey granite. Near the village we observed three or four fields which had been sown with rye, and at a little distance a small wood of firs and birch; in the other parts we could discover nothing but juniper and moss. Beside the hut in which we were lodged, it contained a church and a few scattered cottages. The inhabitants of Cumlin spoke the Swedish language.

The severe frost of the preceding day was succeeded by a sudden thaw, accompanied with rain and sleet; and in the evening a violent hurricane came on; we heard on all sides the cracking of the ice sounding like the explosions of thunder, and which alarmed us with the dread of being detained in so dreadful a spot: for if, as we had reason to apprehend, the ice had been broken up, it could not have been passed in sledges; and a continuance of the thaw for a fortnight at least would have been requisite, before any communication by water could be formed with the continent or neighbouring islands. The wind increasing to a most violent degree towards midnight, and the noise from the bursting of the ice redoubling, we imagined that a considerable delay was unavoidable; and began to inquire whether the inhabitants were furnished with sufficient provisions to supply our wants and their own. We were happy to find, that four cows, a few hogs, and poultry, and a large store of hard bread, which they bake twice in the year, were more than sufficient to remove all apprehensions of famine during a much longer period than we were likely to remain upon the island. Fortunately, however, we did not put these resources to the test: towards morning the wind subsided, and the rents in the ice not appearing dangerous, we were able to continue our route at sun-rise. It was a most delightful day; in the morning the mercury in the thermometer stood at two degrees above freezing point, and at noon rose to five; the sun shone with such brightness, and the weather was so clear and warm, that we might almost have imagined it to have been summer, if we had not been undeceived by the frozen mass around us. On the preceding day the whole scenery was uniformly enveloped with snow, which having been melted, the surface of the Gulf became a pure expanse of ice: the distance to the next post was 35 miles, and much less diversified with islands than the parts which we had passed previous to our arrival at Cumlin. In one place we traversed a level sheet of ice, at least ten miles in length, unbroken with a single rock or island; but as the late storm had produced several apertures, and as the thaw greatly increased, we went on with caution, and were preceded by an inhabitant of Cumlin for our guide, who carried a hatchet and plumbing iron: with the former he occasionally cut the ice, and with the latter he measured its thickness, in order to ascertain whether it was sufficiently strong to support our sledges. In some places he made a considerable circuit to avoid an aperture; often called out to the drivers to keep at some distance from each other; and repeatedly warned them to follow the precise track which he pursued. In this manner he conducted us in about eight hours, and without the least accident, to the isle of Aland.

'Having gratified [their] curiosity at Castelholm', by crawling, like Wraxall, into the ruins of the dungeon where Erik XIV had been imprisoned, they took all night to get across Åland to 'the place of embarkation on the western shore of the island'. Here the water was free of ice, and as no 'decked boat' was available, they continued their journey in two open boats. A sudden storm caught them near the Swedish coast, and they were in grave danger of their lives before finally scrambling ashore near Grisslehamn.

Coxe's account of Finland is an impressive piece of writing. He has a skill which only the best travel writers possess, that of combining factual material with a forward-moving narrative, and he adds to this an elegance and assurance of style. His eye for the picturesque, and appreciation of romantic views reveal him as very much a writer of his time, yet he never loses sight of practical details. It is easy to understand why his *Travels* was so highly regarded.

Matthew Consett

In 1812 *The Edinburgh Review*, in the course of some remarks about travellers to the north of Europe, had this to say about Matthew Consett:

> Mr. Consett would scarcely pardon us, perhaps, if we overlooked his seemly quarto. This gentleman accompanied Sir Henry George Liddell, and Mr. Bower on a trip to Tornea, occasioned by a wager. The gallant trio, in the course of about fifty days, measured over a space of three thousand seven hundred and eighty four miles, and returned, in the same nimble style, with five reindeer and two Lapland shepherdesses in their train! There are several judicious remarks upon cookery in the course of this volume; but the sum of the author's *philosophy* is reserved for the conclusion, where he modestly announces this important and consoling truth, that no-body can 'describe the comfort arising from a *good dinner* and *a bottle of honest port*, so well as he who has been in want of both.'

This summary hardly does justice to Consett. In the letters which make up *A Tour through Sweden, Swedish Lapland, Finland and Denmark* (1789) he certainly betrays the narrowness and prejudice for which the English are often notorious abroad, but he reveals himself also as open-minded and capable of being surprised. He was not, and clearly did not aspire to be, a deep thinker, but his letters reveal in places an honest response to his remarkable experience; he had moved from the sophistications of high society in England to observe a people for the most part very primitive with, it seems, no other preparation for this than a reading of Thomson's *The Seasons*. We often catch him trying to make sense of what he has seen:

> A People that live without exercising the Arts of Agriculture, even the simple ones of ploughing, sowing and planting, affords a singular instance in the present History of the World. Such people are the Natives of Lapland. Ignorant of all the improvements of Life, unknowing in the several embellishments of society, they live, in the interior parts of Lapland, as much as possible in a state of Nature.

Consett was very much of his time in reflecting on the 'state of Nature', and his interest in 'Lapland poetry' similarly links him with aspects of the dawning Romantic movement in England. The Laplanders' poetry gave Consett 'a favourable impression of their taste, and taste most certainly it is, uncorrupted by foreign ideas, and entirely the production of nature'.

The journey took place between 24 May and 17 August, 1786. Consett and his two companions sailed from Shields to Gothenburg, and from there travelled to Stockholm, Uppsala and up the east coast of Sweden, returning by the same route. They stayed their last night in Sweden at a place called Grot, and near there they observed two criminals 'stretched upon the wheel for murder'.

> The morning following, after passing a noble river, we entered Finland. The country here is deep and sandy, and of course barren and unfruitful. The Inhabitants are to appearance rough, and their manners uncultivated to a great degree; but though to a stranger

they appear ignorant, yet they are sufficiently knowing where their own interest is concerned.

Arriving in Finland at midsummer, they achieved one of the greatest of travellers' ambitions:

> At twelve o'clock we saw the Sun in full beauty. The horizon being remarkably clear, gave us a most delightful view of that, *to us*, extraordinary sight. Sir H. G. L. has caused an engraving to be made of this agreeable scene.

This engraving forms the frontispiece of his book (and the cover of the present volume).

The travellers took the opportunity to rest at Tornio, to recover from their transit of Sweden, 'a Journey of eight hundred miles through a country destitute of every comfort and convenience of life'. They attended church, and received 'an invitation from the Judge's lady to drink coffee, the Judge himself then attending the Diet at Stockholm'. This was followed by an invitation to a 'grand ball':

> The Inhabitants of this place, though living as it were at a great distance from polished Society, are far from being an unpolished People. The master of the ceremonies paid us the utmost respect and attention. Being ignorant of their customs, we were, according to the English Phrase, going to take a French leave, but were given to understand that it would be deemed the highest disrespect if we did not particularly salute the Judge's Lady and make a general obeisance to the whole company. With this ceremony, though by no means pleasant to us, we were obliged to comply.

Midsummer Day was one of great festivity in Tornio, with Laplanders flocking in from the surrounding countryside. For them the English travellers were an additional attraction; they crowded their carriage, and peered through their dining-room window. Consett had discovered a great truth about travelling: 'they are also as desirous of seeing us as we can possibly be of observing them'. The day concluded with an adventure:

In the evening a stout Finlander laid his elbows upon the window, and without much ceremony called to us frequently for brandy. We nodded to him as we were drinking our wine, while he continued to repeat his former request in his own language, *Anna ma vino, Hurra Kultana,* 'Dear Gentlemen, give me brandy.' Sir H. with great good nature complied with his request, and gave him two or three glasses which he seemed to enjoy very much, but still he called, *Hurra Kultana.* A few glasses more were given him, which made him drop his elbow from the window, and rather grow shorter. As his legs would not bear him up, he bent his knees against the wall, and by the help of his hands he supported himself, by holding fast by the window post; but still he called, *Hurra Kultana.* Two glasses more were given him, till at length he could say nothing but *Kultana, Kultana,* and gradually sunk from the the window.

When his countrymen who were standing around saw him drop, they took him carefully up and carried him away. Word, however, was soon brought that the man was so ill that they expected his throat would soon be on fire, and if he did not recover before the morning, our post horses would be stopped and our Journey prevented.

Our anxiety was removed in an hour or two's time by the man's appearance once more upon the stage. He came into the yard and began to play several anticks, and to shew us how the Bear dances in the fields.

The Laplanders, he discovered, were very different from the cultured residents of Tornio, whose numbers included 'the much renowned Professor Helands'. He characterised the men as 'muscular and active . . . but perfectly pacific in their tempers', and the women as 'gentle and complaisant'. His account of their language is similarly assured:

> The language of the Laplanders is a harsh and unintelligible Jargon derived from their neighbours, the ancient Inhabitants of Finland. Their voices however are musical and they never require much entreaty to oblige. The few specimens which we possess of Lapland Poetry, give you a favourable impression of their *taste*, and taste most certainly it is, uncorrupted by foreign Ideas, and entirely the production of nature. In the Spectator you have two elegant Odes translated from the language of Lapland . . . I shall make no apology for adding a third. [*See Appendix 2.*]

'With respect to religion,' Consett writes, 'I am afraid that the Laplanders have yet much to learn':

> Many superstitious customs still remain to proclaim the darkness of their minds. Augury and witchcraft make a part of their belief; they still whisper to their Reindeer when they undertake a Journey, and address their ancient Idols for the increase and safety of their flocks. You have heard no doubt of their conjuring Drums . . .
>
> This Instrument is of an oval form, made of the bark of the fir, pine, or birch-tree, one end of which is covered with a sort of parchment dressed from the Rein-deer skin. This is loaded with brass rings artfully fastened to it. The Conjurer than beats it upon his breast with a variety of frantic postures. After this he besmears it with blood, and draws upon it rude figures of various

kinds. When he has gone through all his manœuvres, he informs his credulous audience what they wish to know, which he says was communicated to him during the paroxism of his attitudes.

Consett describes the fishing – especially salmon fishing – and the reindeer; a whole letter is devoted to the rich variety of game birds, with illustrations of several of them (later engraved by a fellow Northumbrian, the young Thomas Bewick). He is especially knowledgeable about gun dogs. He describes the features, dress, and ordinary habits of the Laplanders with great care; the following paragraph is only one example:

> The Laplander is very dexterous in making utensils of wood. He is his own carpenter and boat-builder. I was not a little surprized, in a tent of wandering Lap-landers, to find the cheese which they make of the rein-deer's milk curiously impressed with a wooden instrument such as is commonly used in the English Dairies. They fasten their boards together, when they make their boats or other moveables, with Twigs or the Nerves of the rein-deer. The women also make use of the latter as a substitute for thread in sewing. The fe-male Laplanders shew great ingenuity in embroidering their Garments with brass-wire, tin, or any other gaudy ornament. They take much delight in adorning their heads, neck, and shoulders with glass beads, &c. and are very fanciful in their girdles which are embroidered and fringed with large tufts at the two extremes and tied in large knots; this they look upon as the greatest ornament of their dress.

The Edinburgh Review was perfectly correct in reporting that the travellers on their return had two Lapp girls with them. Consett adds an appendix to his book describing these girls, Sigree and Anea, and the way in which they deported themselves at Ravensworth Castle, the Liddells' ancestral home: 'instead of their Lapland mountains, you would have imagined their education had been in the Drawing room'. They were so close to the state of Nature that it never occurred to them to suspect their hosts' motives; they were for Consett the actual embodiment of natural goodness:

> Though the untutored minds of these Girls could never have been taught any of the sublimer virtues or impressed with a proper sense of Gratitude, yet from all these circumstances it is evident that they possessed it in all its purity.

Such transportations were not unknown to late eighteenth-century England; they were a sort of counterpart to foreign travel. Marilyn Butler has described this phenomenon:

> the search for purity often took the form of a journey into the remote. The settings of poems, plays, paintings and even novels evoked a condition of society that was primitive and pre-social, in contrast to the luxuriousness which was seen as the characteristic of contemporary life in Western Europe. Heroes from simpler worlds visited civilisation for the purpose of making adverse comparisons.

Only a few years before a young South Sea islander called Omai had been brought to London, and quickly became both a curiosity and a celebrity, welcomed into fashionable society. In the same way the girls from Lapland

> were received in this country as great curiosities and visited by all ranks of People. And probably they were as curious to see others, as others were to see them.

After their stay in England the girls returned home, and were received by the Swedish king on the way. Consett recorded that it turned out well for the reindeer too, which 'since their arrival in England have bred, and are likely to become very prolific'. Unfortunately, his optimism proved to be ill-founded: 'every animal perished during a severe winter a few years later, through neglect upon the part of those to whom they had been left in charge'.

It must be admitted, in conclusion, that Consett's *Tour* is a disappointment. After describing the grand ball in Tornio he hardly mentions anything that he did, but prefers to give an *account* of Lapland. This was the tradition of this sort of book: the object was to show not so much how the traveller had responded to his experiences as what information he had gained about the places visited. Sadly, this information is of only limited interest to a modern reader.

Edward Daniel Clarke

Matthew Consett was young, fashionable and wealthy, and had gone to Finland for a bet; Edward Daniel Clarke, by contrast, was a scientist travelling as a salaried tutor. He had become interested in natural science while still an undergraduate at Cambridge, and he began his collection of mineralogical specimens while on a tour of England in 1791. During the early 1790s he became tutor in a series of great houses, and this enabled him to travel widely in Italy and Germany at no expense to himself. In 1798 he was approached by John Marten Cripps, who had just come into a large fortune at the age of nineteen, and 'was desirous of placing himself under the guidance and instruction of Mr. Clarke for three years, in the meritorious hope of supplying the defects of an indifferent education'. Clarke was now a Fellow of Jesus College; Cripps enrolled as commoner there, and the following year they set off on what was intended as a six-month journey to northern Europe. They were away for three and a half years.

Travelling with them were Thomas Malthus, who had just published his famous *Essay on the Principle of Population*, and William Otter, later Bishop of Chichester and also Clarke's biographer. These two were not equal to the pace, and after a month separated to take a more leisurely tour, which, as Otter wrote, 'could be comprehended within the extended limits of a long vacation'. Otter and Malthus actually got as far as Russia; it is most unfortunate that the final volume of Malthus's Scandinavian journal, which must have described this part of his journey, is lost – and possibly was lost by Clarke. Cripps, in contrast to these two, was indefatigable: 'He would go to the mountains of the moon,' Clarke wrote to his mother, 'if I would consent to accompany him. I never had a more active, useful, or pleasant companion in travels.' Cripps was unfailingly devoted to his tutor, in sickness and in health.

Their route was via Hamburg to Copenhagen, then to Gothenburg, Halby and Stockholm. They travelled up the Swedish coast by way of Sundsvall to Tornio, then north to the mouth of the Muonio river, which they followed all the way to its source at Enontekiö. From there they returned by a more easterly route to Tornio and Oulu, took a boat from Vaasa to Umeå, and continued their journey to Norway. They eventually returned to Stockholm, and set off on a winter journey across the ice to Turku where they stayed for about two weeks before taking the coastal route to St Petersburg.

Clarke's account of Finland is justly famous, and to make selections from it does it an injustice. To give some idea of the scale and comprehensiveness of his work I have reprinted in Appendix 4 the ample 'General Statement of Contents' of the first phase of the *Travels*, which gives in Clarke's own words the context of the extracts which follow, and at the same time indicates the full range of his interests and observations.

LAPLAND AND NORTHERN OSTROBOTHNIA

They entered Finland at Tornio early in July, 1799, and Clarke immediately perceived a change:

> We were now drawing near to the dwellings of a race of men very different in character and morals from the *Swedes*, namely, the *Finlanders*; and as this race prevails

among the inhabitants, a greater vivacity of spirit, a more irascible disposition, and a propensity to criminal actions, begins to be manifested. This change becomes remarkably conspicuous to those who pass round the *northern* extremity of the Gulph; but the river *Torneå* has been generally considered as the boundary separating the two people.

He returns to this distinction later, stating that at the head of the Gulf of Bothnia 'whenever the *Finns* were mentioned in conversation, the inhabitants shake their heads, ascribing to them, or to their influence, all deeds of anger, lust, violence and drunkenness'.

Despite these initial impressions, they found Tornio comfortable enough:

Of a town so little known as *Torneå*, one would wish to convey an accurate idea by description. It consists of two principal streets, nearly half an *English* mile in length. The houses are all of wood. After what has been said of its civilized external aspect, it ought only to be considered as less barbarous, in its appearance, than the generality of towns in the *north* of *Sweden*. It must not be inferred, that there is the slightest similitude between this place and one of the towns in *England*. If it were possible to transport the reader, now engaged in perusing this description, into the midst of *Torneå*, the first impression upon his mind would be, that he was surrounded by a number of fagot-stacks, and piles of timber, heaped by the water-side for exportation, rather than inhabited houses. The inn, however, a very good one for this part of the world, was clean and comfortable; and, in proof of it, we had no necessity to make use of our own sheets for the beds, which is not often the case, even in the best towns upon the continent. The dinner, which, without any previous notice, was placed before us, will shew something of the manner and condition of the inhabitants. It consisted of *pickled salmon, chocolate milk,* by way of *soup, pancakes,* a kind of cakes called *diet-bread, rye biscuit,* and *reindeer cheese.* For our beverage, we had bottled *Swedish* beer, not unlike *Cambridge* ale, and *Moselle* and *Pontac* wines.

The meal was followed by tea, 'served as in England', but they were allowed coffee only on a promise of secrecy, since it was 'a prohibited article'. In a letter written to a college friend Clarke is a little more forthcoming about his activities in Tornio: 'We have had our tea, and a game of romps with some Lapland lasses – I am preparing to have a dance with them.' To his mother he emphasised different enthusiasms: 'How happy I am! Can I believe? – am I dreaming? – pinch my nose! To tread within the arctic! – only fancy!'

As they left Tornio to follow the river north, Clarke wrote, 'we found our company to consist of five persons, besides boatmen; including the Lapland and Swedish interpreters, an English servant, and ourselves'. Mr Pipping, son of a Tornio merchant, had volunteered his services as a Lappish and Finnish interpreter; he knew the land well, as he had associated with Laplanders all his life, and had travelled several times to the North Cape. His expertise went far beyond interpreting, and he proved to be indispensable. As they planned to stock the boat with provisions, he said that 'he had a companion who would cater for us, and often find plenty of food'. This companion turned out to be his dog. During the journey Pipping was hailed everywhere 'as a person of much consequence', and the travellers 'gave him the appellation of "King Pipping"'.

Between Tornio and Enontekiö there were 107 rapids to be negotiated. Clarke writes with admiration of the skill and hardiness of the boatmen, who used not oars but poles to take the boat up the rapids. To Clarke it seemed that the boatmen were rather like the post-horses at the post-ing stations, 'relays being appointed at certain stages'. They seem not to have been officially regulated: when there was no relay available at the end of one station, the men from Ylitornio volunteered to work a second shift for two glasses of brandy each.

The picture which Clarke gives of the region north of Tornio is a most attractive one of well-cultivated riverside fields, with a seemingly never-ending sequence of 'pictur-esque views' of pretty farms and villages. They took what-ever accommodation they could find on the way. Sometimes they stayed at parsonages, but more commonly at small farms. Almost everywhere Clarke comments on the neat-ness of the houses and the cleanliness of the interiors. The journey was not without surprises, such as on the the night they reached Korpikylä:

> not being able to find a human being, we began to sus-pect that the place was deserted; when our boatman, knowing better where to look for the people, opened the door of one of the little *steam-baths*, for all the world like a cow-house, and out rushed men, women, and children, stark-naked, with dripping locks and scorched skins, and began rolling about upon the grass. Here we passed the night, in a room with windows like small port-holes of a ship.

Clarke faced many unavoidable dangers during his time in Scandinavia, but here he actually chose to risk his life:

One of the Falls of the *Torneå* occurs near *Korpikylå*; it is called *Matha Koski*, and is really a clamorous and turbulent cascade. Having enquired if any of them ever ventured down this cataract in their canoes, they answered in the affirmative: upon which the author expressed an inclination to accompany any of them who would descend with him; and two men gladly volunteered their services, desiring him only to sit perfectly still in the boat, without moving either hand or foot, and not attempt to interfere with its management. The rest all crowded to the side of the river, as the boat was pushed off towards the middle of the stream. Presently it was caught by the force of the descending current, and carried with indescribable velocity, amidst foam and rocks, to the bottom of the Fall; the two men guiding it with their poles only, but with surprising dexterity, until it reached with safety the calmer surface, when all those on shore set up a shout of triumph.

At the minister's house at Ylitornio, which had appeared to be a haven of elegance, and where Clarke had romantically designated 'the parsonage, *Parnassus,* the minister's daughters the *Muses,* and Secretary *Swamberg* a representative of *Apollo',* he had a rude awakening:

The author, after a conversation with Mr. *Swamberg* respecting the proper route to be observed in penetrating farther towards the *North*, ascended to a chamber prepared for his reception; and being overcome by weariness and illness, was surprised and glad to find a cleanly-looking *English* bed, with cotton curtains, white as snow. This being the case, he incautiously resolved not to use his own; sending the servants away, to sleep in the village. He had not been long in the bed, where the *mosquitos* proved sufficiently troublesome, when he saw a dark moving spot upon the white curtain, which proved to be a most enormous species of *bug*. Having removed it, and hoping it might be a solitary vagrant, he ventured to lie down again. Soon after, he saw three more, of a size hardly to be credited; when, starting up, what words can express his astonishment and disgust, in beholding myriads, moving in all directions over his bed and body. Heaps of them adhered together, like bees about to swarm: and mingled with these nauseous insects, there were other vermin, of a description so filthy and abominable as to be nameless in every civilized society. In this deplorable situation, there was nothing for it, but to strip naked, and rush into the river: after which, returning once more, and finding in an antechamber a huge bear-skin pelisse belonging to the minister, he wrapped himself in the fur, and remained upon the floor until the family was roused.

Ever ready to adjust his impressions, at the next place they stopped, 'Tavonico' (perhaps Taroniemi), Clarke felt that 'it may be well to mention the extraordinary cleanliness of this farm-house'.

The bugs were an intermittent occurrence; the mosquitoes they had always with them. Hardly a day passed without the travellers, and especially their servants, being tormented and driven near to desperation. It was a subject which every summer traveller in Finland encountered and dramatised; the *Edinburgh Review* notice of Acerbi's *Travels* complained that 'the constant recurrence of the mosquitoes becomes almost as troublesome and fatiguing to the reader, as they were to the travellers'. When all else failed they reluctantly adopted the local technique, and smeared themselves with tar. Despite these difficulties and distractions, Clarke's scientific curiosity and his powers of observation were unaffected. More unexpected is the sense of religious awe which came to him as he contemplated scenes where man had made no mark. He felt 'a stillness which is quite awful; it is the unbroken silence of Nature left entirely to herself'. In another scene he felt that 'Man seems to be an intruder, for the first time, in the midst of solitudes that have never been trodden by any human foot.'

After one 'pedestrian excursion' while the boat was being poled up a cataract, an astonishing sight met their eyes when they boarded again:

> the extraordinary scene exhibited baffled all power of verbal description; and even painting would give but an imperfect idea of it. Its formality was not less striking than its great magnificence. Let the Reader imagine himself at the extremity of an area whose form is that of a *Greek stadium*, two *English* miles in length, and a quarter of a mile wide: the ground of this area occupied by the most rapid and pellucid river, flowing placidly towards him; all the lower parts of the immense *coilon*, for the seats, covered with *wild roses, weeping birch, downy willows, aspens, alders,* &c.; all the upper parts, with high-towering *pines,* standing in tiers one above another, and, at a distance, seeming like crowded rows of spectators in this vast natural amphitheatre. To add to the splendour of the scene, the sun, reflected in dazzling brightness by the water, was shining in all its glory.

In this paean to nature the romantic and the classical seem to join together.

In Muonio they were treated to a performance of a Lapland song, 'Let us drive the wolves', an offering very much less sophisticated than the verses which Addison had published for the readers of *The Spectator*. After a 'long and treacherous journey' to a Chief's tent, their host disposed of Clarke's gift of brandy in one swig, 'uttered a most fearful yell', and seemed as if he would bite the listeners:

> The boy also, our former guide, sang the same ditty. During their singing, they strained their lungs so as to cause a kind of spasmodic convulsion of the chest, which produced a noise like the braying of an ass.

The travellers ate well, with abundant game and fish, and farm produce regularly available. Being English, they drew the line at going native to the extent of eating raw fish; on one occasion they had bought a salmon weighing twenty-one pounds:

> Mr. *Pipping*, cutting a slice, began to eat it raw; and this not owing to hunger or to any want of what are considered refined manners in this country, but as the greatest possible delicacy. He endeavoured often, afterwards, to prevail upon us to do the same; laughing at our prejudices, and saying, if we knew what a luxury raw salmon affords, when quite fresh, we should not hesitate.

Throughout Lapland this fish was in abundant supply, but repeatedly the travellers had to stop in order to 'dress [their] salmon'. They could summon no enthusiasm for piimä, a cultured sour milk still popular in Finland today, whereas the Laplanders were 'so fond of it that they talk of this beverage as our common people do of beer; saying that it is, at the same time, both "meat and drink"'. At least the wild berries suited the English palate; the Arctic cloudberry was not only delicious but, as events were to prove, a life-saver. Clarke was astonished that the 'natives' could thrive on their chosen diet:

Yet how feeble did the stoutest of us appear, when opposed to them! We never saw stronger or healthier men anywhere; the principal article of whose diet is sour fermented *milk* like the Koumyss of the *Calmucks*. The quantity of flesh which, together with strong drink, constitutes the food of an *Englishman*, and without which he fancies he cannot work, would enervate and destroy an *Arctic* farmer; who labours more, when it is necessary, and with less fatigue, than any of the *London* coal-heavers; taking no other sustenance, for days together, than a little biscuit, half of which consists of the bark of trees, washed down by *pïma*.

The punishing schedule which had been too much for Otter and Malthus, now affected Clarke's own health, and he lay weak and sick in the bottom of their boat, as it was poled up the endless series of rapids. As they arrived in Enontekiö an astonishing sight met their eyes – a scene which might have come from one of Evelyn Waugh's travel books:

> We had no sooner landed, and were proceeding towards the dwelling of the *Minister*, than we perceived this reverend missionary coming towards us, followed by half-a-dozen *dogs* and two tame *pigs*: he was dressed in a long frock of black bombazeen reaching to his feet, and advanced smoking his tobacco pipe.

This was Pastor Erik Grape; he 'addressed us in *Latin,* desiring that we would make use of his house as if it were our own'. With him Clarke developed one of the warmest friendships of all his travels.

Clarke was now seriously ill with fever and loss of appetite. He languished for many days at the parsonage house until, one day, two of Pastor Grape's young children brought home 'two or three gallons of the fruit of the *Cloudberry* or

Rubus Chamaemorus', with unexpected – indeed, miraculous – results:

> Little did the author dream of the blessed effects he was to experience by tasting of the offering brought by these little children . . . [H]is fever rapidly abated, his spirits and appetite were restored; – and, when sinking under a disorder so obstinate that it seemed to be incurable, the blessings of health were restored to him, where he had reason to believe that he should have found his grave. The symptoms of amendment were almost simultaneous, after eating of these berries.

He was still too weak to be able to go with Cripps to view the midnight sun from Nonainen, the nearest mountain. He spent the time writing up his journal; a visiting Lapp and his wife watched him writing, 'both regarding with wonder an employment wholly inexplicable to them'. The 'Extraordinary Proposal made to the Author', mentioned in the General Statement, followed this:

> As soon as he had laid down his pen, the same *Laplander*, pointing to his wife and to the bed, made a free tender of her person and charms, in the most unequivocal manner. Upon mentioning this circumstance to Mr. *Grape*, he said, that the *Lapps* consider it as a great honour, and as a propitious event, when any stranger will accept of an offer of this kind. The whole race of *Laplanders* are pigmies. This man was about four feet and a half in height; his hair, straight and dark, hung scantily down the sides of his lean and swarthy face: his eyes were almost sunk in his head. His wife, with a shrivelled skin, and a complexion of one uniform copper colour, was even more dwarfish than her husband. Her features resembled those of the *Chinese*: high cheek-bones; little sore eyes,

widely separated from each other; a wide mouth; and a flat nose. Her hair was tressed up, and entirely concealed beneath a skull-cap: her teeth black: and between her lips she held a tobacco-pipe, smoking; the tube of which was so short, that the kindled weed threatened to scorch the end of her nose. A more unsightly female, or with less of the human form in appearance, can hardly be conceived. Indeed, both man and woman, if exhibited in a *menagerie* of wild beasts, might be considered as the long-lost link between man and ape.

On 28 July they went to church. The sermon was 'an extemporaneous harangue; but delivered in a tone of voice so elevated, that the worthy pastor seemed to labour as if he would burst a blood-vessel. He continued exerting his lungs in this manner during one hour and twenty minutes, as if his audience had been stationed upon the top of a distant mountain.' Despite the volume, 'which made our ears ring', the sexton walked around with a large pole to arouse the sleeping congregation. Pastor Grape later explained to Clarke that he could not appear 'feeble and impotent' to his parishioners, since 'the preacher was always estimated . . . by the strength and power of his voice'.

Clarke had achieved some fame in college at Cambridge by constructing a balloon, which was launched from the college grounds with a kitten on board. He promised that he would launch one in the parish, 'with a view of bringing together the dispersed families of the *wild Laplanders*, who are so rarely seen collected in any number'. With the Pastor's approval and cooperation the balloon was constructed and tested in the church. It was inflated

by burning beneath it a ball of cotton steeped in alcohol. It was seventeen feet in height, and nearly fifty in circumference; and being all of white satin-paper, set off with scarlet hangings, made rather a splendid appearance.

The congregation waited all afternoon after a first, abortive attempt to launch the balloon in strong winds, drowning their disappointment in brandy. Finally

the volant orb rose majestically into the atmosphere, to the great astonishment, and evidently to the dismay, of all the *Lapps;* for their *rein-deer* taking fright, scampered off in all directions, followed by the owners, who were not a whit less alarmed themselves. The balloon, after soaring over the Source of the *Muonio,* descended into the Lake, where, rolling about upon the surface of the water, we expected to see it presently immersed; but, to our surprise, notwithstanding all the moisture it had imbibed, it rose again to a considerable height, and then fell. When this exhibition was over, which, for reasons we could not explain, gave rather uneasiness, than pleasure, to the *Laplanders,* we hoisted the large *kite* we had made for Mr. *Grape's* children; at sight of which, the *Lapps* were beyond measure delighted. Both old and young, men, women, and children, all were alike transported, expressing their joy by capering and squeaking, each coming in his turn to lay hold upon the string: when, finding that it was pulled by the *kite,* they burst into loud fits of laughter, and would have remained the whole night amused by the sight it afforded. Even the worthy Pastor himself said it should be carefully preserved; as it would be useful to him to use as a signal for calling the *Lapps* together, when he might wish to bring them to his house. Having succeeded much more to the satisfaction of the *Lapps* with our *kite* than with our *balloon*, they began to kiss our hands, and were willing to grant us any favour. The rest of the night, therefore, was past in mirth and rejoicing: we had races in sledges, drawn by *rein-deer* over the smooth grass; and amused ourselves by riding upon the backs of these animals; being always outstripped by the *Lapps*, who were as much delighted with our awkwardness as we were with the strange gestures and manners of this very singular people.

'I do not intend to turn back till I have dipped in the icy sea,' Clarke had written to Malthus, but Pastor Grape dissuaded the invalid from these North Cape ambitions. Invalid or not, he was not one to retrace his footsteps, and he decided 'to cross over, by means of a chain of lakes, from the *Muonio* to the *Aunis* river, and thence descend the *Kiemi* river to the gulph of *Bothnia*'. It was time to travel on:

Wednesday July 31. – Towards the evening of this day, we left *Enontekis*. Mr. *Grape*, his wife, his brother-in-law, and all the other members of his family, attended us to the water-side. The farewell affected us deeply. The thoughts of leaving for ever, and in such a solitude, so good a man, were very painful. His little children hung about our knees; and, as we parted, tears were shed on all sides. In the last view we caught of them, we saw the venerable missionary, surrounded by his relatives, waving his hat in the air, in token of *adieu*.

It was nearly twenty years later, not long before his death, that Clarke wrote up this part of his *Travels*:

and, at this distance of time, notwithstanding all the subsequent images that have filled the mind under other impressions of grief or gladness, the sight we had of this affecting group remains as fresh upon the memory as when it was actually beheld.

After the dash for the North Cape had failed, a more leisurely regime was adopted, partly because Clarke's health had been permanently damaged. They followed two rivers: the Ounasjoki through Kittelä to Roveniemi, and then the Kemijoki as far as the Gulf of Bothnia. The itinerary is given in the General Statement. So unaccustomed were the natives to seeing any sort of stranger that at times their amazement is reminiscent of scenes in Swift's *Gulliver's Travels*, for example in this episode which occurred near Pallastunturi:

> The family of our *Lappish* host, at *Kuru*, was very large: they all came, as it was usual in places where we rested for the night, to see us undress. We could not repress their curiosity without giving them offence: therefore we suffered them to remain in the room; where they behaved with great gravity, whispering to each other, and making some remarks upon every article of our apparel. Our boots or shoes were always examined with great surprise: but if we took off our stockings, or put on a night-cap, the wonder was heightened; for having no idea of their utility, and perhaps not thinking them ornamental, we had always some questions to answer, as to the meaning of such a ceremony. *Pipping* undertook to explain matters to our visitants; entertaining them with his strange stories of the country where all these marvels were manufactured; and now and then, cracking his jokes with the women, who would be prying into every thing, a momentary mirth was excited.

There were several similar episodes of native incomprehension, such as when the Laplanders showed no understanding of the concept of money.

As they followed the river south of Pallastunturi Clarke, looking back, savoured the prospect in unexpected terms:

> the new-mown banks of this pellucid river, sloping to the water's edge, garnished with weeping *birch* and the most elegant *fir trees*, had rather the appearance of grounds set off by studied and tastely art, than by the wilderness of uncultivated nature.

They stopped at a farm here, where they had some of their best and worst Lapland experiences. They were pestered by '[v]ermin of the most unpleasant description', and the farmhouse, with no windows and heated by a 'prodigious stove, like a brick kiln', was intolerably hot. There was no escape: they were either to be smoked out, or eaten alive by mosquitoes. On the other hand they had a princely dinner, with a huge bowl of rich cream,

> unequalled, as to its excellence, in any other part of the world. We had, besides, mutton, sweet as that of the *Shetland* Isles; to which there is not the slightest resemblance in meat bearing the same name in *England*. And to heighten the luxury afforded by these viands, our feast was accompanied by the sound of the only musical instrument we had yet heard in all *Lapland*. Poets might have believed that *Orpheus*, in his long wanderings through the regions of the *Hyperboreans*, had left his lyre among them; for it was, in fact the *Lyre* of the antient *Finns*, with *five* strings, adapted to the *five* notes peculiar to all their *music* and *poetry*.

As they passed Rovaniemi Clarke recorded his feelings on leaving the Arctic circle:

> A sudden feeling of exultation, at the successful termination of our expedition within the *Frigid Zone*,

prompted us to stand up in the boat, with our hats off, as we crossed once more this *polar* boundary. We looked back towards the regions we had traversed, unmindful of the toils, the trials, and privations, to which we had been exposed; not being altogether insensible of a contending emotion of regret, in the consciousness that we should see those scenes no more.

They followed the Kemijoki to Tervola, where they hired boats to take them to Kemi. For Clarke it was now farewell to the solitude of Lapland, and he describes appreciatively the changed landscape:

Here forests no longer crowd and darken the sides of the river; the land appears like a fine cultivated garden; farms, continually succeeding to each other in an uninterrupted series, cover the shores with cheerful dwellings.

As they approached Kemi the church came into view, and he was astonished at the 'anomaly of a stately *Grecian* structure upon the borders of *Lapland*'. 'Designed in good taste, but ill-executed' was his judgement, but he conceded that they 'could not call to mind a village in all *Great Britain* with so magnificent a church as this'.

Clarke felt that they were fortunate to have arrived at Kemi during the annual fair:

It was a gay scene: the boats passing to and from the isle to the shore, and the crowd assembled upon the little island, formed a very pleasant *coup d'oeil*. The church service had just ended as we landed. A vast throng of peasants were filling all the boats, to go over to the island. Seeing this, we stepped into one of the boats, and were speedily conducted into the midst of the jovial multitude. Of what nature the church service had been, they were very ill-calculated to inform us: by much the greater part of the men were very drunk, shouting, singing, and romping with their favourite lasses. Great allowance must be made for the joyous season of this annual festival; but these were almost all of them *Finlanders*; and the *Finns* are notoriously of a livelier and more profligate disposition then the *Swedes*.

Clarke wrote warmly of the character and attainments of the minister, who provided them with useful travelling information, and gave them 'many rare plants which he had collected'.

From Kemi they hired carts to drive them to Tornio, where they drank tea with Mr Pipping's father, a merchant there. Returning to Kemi, they said a final farewell to Mr Pipping, which 'depressed all our spirits', before heading south for Oulu. While they lingered in Oulu they at last met Acerbi, the Italian traveller, whose tracks they had crossed more than once, and whose own *Travels* would be published many years before Clarke's. A Swedish resident, Baron Silferhielm, 'desired that we should use his house as our own, while we staid'. Another gentleman invited them to one of the concerts instituted by Acerbi. The contrast with Lapland was very marked:

> After the concert was ended, we supped with the Baron. His entertainment was sumptuous, and the company numerous. *Acerbi* was placed at the head of the table; entertaining every body by his lively and engaging conversation. Among the ladies present, there was one of uncommon beauty, whom every body addressed by the name of *Albertina*. Many of the gentlemen, as it is customary in this and in some other countries, instead of being seated, walked round the table. The

mention of these circumstances may appear trifling; but to us, the sudden transition, from scenes of savage life, was so extraordinary, that it seemed to be the effect of a dream. Within a very short space of time we had exchanged the wildernesses of *Lapland* for the luxuries of polished society; brilliant lustres, supporting *English* patent-lamps, being substituted for burning splinters; a magnificent saloon for a narrow, contracted, and smoky cabin; French confectionery for bread made of birch-bark and chopped straw; the most costly dainties for raw or dried fish and flesh; beauty and wit and wine, for ugliness and stupidity and *pïma*. Wonder not then, Reader, that we have been tempted to tell thee how we supped with Baron *Silferhielm,* at *Uleåborg!*

Heading south from Oulo they had intended stopping at Kempele, 'but the accommodations were too bad even for persons accustomed to Lapland fare'. Going on to Liminka meant travelling after sunset, and as a result Clarke caught a violent cold which developed into a dangerous fever. True to his admiration of the Finnish diet, he tried to relieve this 'by adhering solely to a diet of pïma; but it increased the disorder'. The journey over sandy roads through marshy land was slow, and the only diversion was a particularly hideous one:

Just before we reached *Oljocki,* an open space in the forest, cleared for the purpose, exhibited, upon three wheels, the mangled carcase of a miscreant *Finn*, who, in a fit of intoxication, had cut off a woman's head with an axe. His head was placed upon one wheel, his right hand upon another; and his body, dressed according to the habit of his nation, in a white frock with a yellow sash, rested upon a third, in the middle, between the

80

other two . . . Amidst the gloom and solitude of the forest, where the silence was that of death itself, it was indeed a sight that spoke terrible things.

The scene is illustrated with a graphic engraving.

At Olkijoki they 'quitted the main road' to seek medical assistance for Clarke in Raahe, 'a new and neat town', and 'in a flourishing state'. A German quack offered a new cure, 'painting the inside of the throat, by means of a camel's hair brush, dipped in a kind of green paint'. Clarke felt that this treatment was likely to be worse than the disease, so paid him off and travelled on.

The country south of this place was as beautiful as the County of *Surrey,* which it resembled. A wide prospect of rich cultivated country extended on every side: in the midst of it appeared large farms, and husbandmen everywhere busy, with their families, getting in the harvest.

Ostrobothnia, he wrote,

is the most fertile part of the *Swedish* dominions. The farmers are remarkable for their neatness in agriculture: the land, after they have finished ploughing and harrowing, looks like a well-cultivated garden.

In Kokkola 'as usual, we observed two churches; one for the mercantile inhabitants; the other for the peasants'. Among the crops he noted were wheat, potatoes, barley, rye, hops, and turnips. Everything in this area seemed prosperous, and the people well-fed and industrious; 'the busy scenes of active life, which we everywhere saw, denoted a thriving population.'

As they approached Uusikaarlepyy Clarke was struck by

the most pleasing and picturesque appearance of any town in *Sweden* or *Finland*. Its churches and light spires towering above the other buildings, and the whole rising above a winding river, in the midst of beautiful clumps of trees and hop-grounds, producing as fine hops as any in *England,* delighted us.

Close up, however, the town was less attractive, the streets 'narrow and ill-paved'.

They were advised not to attempt the passage to Sweden until they got to Vaasa, so they continued by land, observing as they left the town, 'the finest plantations of *tobacco* we had ever seen'. At 'Wickas' they 'met some of the prettiest girls we had ever seen, returning from church in carts'. Vaasa, with its 'romantic situation', appeared to be deserted. For their journey across the Gulf to Umeå they

determined to venture in the small open boats of the country, according to the custom of the peasants, who run in them from one small island to another, as the weather serves. Pheasants here were so common, that they were sent to our table both at dinner and supper. A pin-maker lodged in a room opposite to ours; and the noise of his wheels was a proof of his industry, as it continued, without any intermission, the whole of the time we staid. Sounds more musical attracted our notice to a performer on an instrument called a *Hummer*, or Half-harp, something like a guitar . . . The instrument being placed on a table, the performer, playing upon the four strings, made use of two quills pressing the strings in different parts with one of the quills, while he struck four of them with the other.

A few hours after embarking they were driven ashore by a contrary wind on Björkö, where Clarke was delighted to find several rare plants, 'curious, owing to their situation', as well as masses of wild raspberries, strawberries and redcurrants. They spent two days and nights on the island, staying at the village, and Clarke took enormous interest in every aspect of island life, including the local economy. This is, in fact, the first reference in English to what is now a UNESCO World Heritage site: Qvarken.

In the village was kept

> the public barge, a vessel constructed of the trunks of unhewn trees, belonging to all the natives in common; but, like the proud *Gondola* of the *Doge* and Commonwealth of *Venice*, laid up in state and security, to be used only on great occasions.

Clarke's unscheduled visit clearly ranked as a great occasion, since on 1 September 'we were summoned to embark in the public barge' which 'with difficulty, contained our little wagon and a large hog which the natives were desirous of conveying to Umeå for sale'. And so, accompanied by a pig, Clarke and his party departed from Finland.

THE ÅLAND ARCHIPELAGO, TURKU AND SOUTHERN FINLAND

From Umeå Clarke and Cripps struck across country to Norway. Their travels brought them eventually, in mid-November, to Stockholm, where they stayed for a month of recuperation and study. On December 14 they set off for Finland again. At Grisslehamn they waited for six days, in miserable conditions, for a favourable wind. The first attempt to set sail very nearly ended their travels for good. In a letter to a Cambridge friend Clarke wrote:

Now, their boats are not accustomed to take large carriages; neither are they fit for it. You might as well put to sea in a saucer, and if the saucer is half-filled with snow, and very shallow, you will have some idea of the Finland passage boats.

Clarke gives a detailed, vivid and terrifying account of the storm they survived, when 'all hope was gone' and '[a]ll subordination lost' among the sailors. A telling detail is that when all hope had been abandoned, Clarke's last action was to ask for Cripps to be lashed to an oar.

When they eventually set sail again it seemed that they had escaped death only to encounter it again; 'we knew not how our escape was effected,' wrote Clarke, 'being quite stupefied and numbed by our dreadful situation'. From Eckerö they continued over the ice; a process of island-hopping took them to Kastelholm, where Clarke was more interested in the red granite and the 'terra-cotta of the bricks' than in anecdotes about Erik XIV's incarceration. Soon after this they had to part company with their carriage, which was too heavy for the December ice, and they hired a horse-drawn sledge. It was several weeks before they were reunited with the carriage, but travelling without it proved to be a liberation. 'Never was any mode of travelling more delightful', Clarke wrote, 'than this of the open sledge.' He was quickly convinced 'of the folly and inconvenience of being pent in close carriages'. The Swedish spoken on these islands was, he claimed, 'so near the English, that a servant of our own country, who travelled with us, was able to understand and sometimes converse with the natives'. On Vårdö, at 'the hovel called the Post-house', they had just taken possession of the only room when Clarke was astonished to see thirteen members of the family, 'who had been piled in tiers one above another, as in a ship's cabin', tumble naked onto the floor and begin 'altogether the business of their brief toilette'. They then got dressed, the men lit their pipes, and breakfast was handed round: 'a portion of black biscuit, with about two ounces of fresh butter', preceded by a dram:

> It was rather new, to see mothers with children at their breasts disengage their tender infants from the nipple, to pour down their little throats a portion of the dram which came to the mother's share; but still more remarkable to see these young dram-drinkers lick their lips, roll their eyes about, and stretch out their puny hands, as craving more; showing how accustomed they were to this beverage. Perhaps the practice may explain the frequency of dwarfs in the Northern countries of *Europe*.

The thirty or so pages which Clarke devotes to his experiences in getting from Vårdö to Kumlinge are an adventure story in themselves: added to the Arctic temperatures, the treacherous ice, a hurricane, and extraordinarily roundabout routes (eventually via Sottunga) were added separation from of the carriage, parting from Cripps, and, already deserted by his interpreter, being abandoned alone on the ice. Rather than retell the experience, Clarke transcribed this portion of his work '*verbatim*. . . as it occurs in his own manuscript journal'.

New Year's Eve Clarke records in memorable detail:

> As we continued to advance across the more open sea, the ice became stronger: and being now at a considerable distance from any land, the prospect widened on all sides, and became at every instant more desolate and appalling. The wind had carried off every particle of snow; and we journeyed for many miles over a surface clear and transparent as glass. It was the last day of

the eighteenth century; which made me push forward with spirit and vigour, that, at least, I might terminate the most extraordinary adventure of my life, together with the most remarkable period of it, in some place where I could lay my head and not remain benighted on the frozen surface of an inhospitable sea. At mid-day, I halted to distribute some slight refreshment among our guides. As I served out to them their allowance of biscuit and *Swedish* brandy, they all stood bare-headed, and said grace. What a scene, for such solemnity!

Clarke gives only the briefest, factual account of Kumlinge; there was, at least, an inn, where he found his 'long-lost Friend and Companion'. Cripps, who with their guide had travelled by a different route, had been holed up in this 'black and miserable dungeon' for a week. They left the next day – the first day of 1800 – for Brändö. The journey was exciting but also very hazardous, with the skill and courage of the guides continually saving them from disaster. Here they saw the remarkable sight of the congregation leaving church, and dispersing in every direction over the ice:

Upwards of an hundred sledges, to which wild and beautiful horses were harnessed, were seen presently in motion; and they might be said, like so many vessels, to be literally *'getting under weigh;'* for they all took to the sea; where, being extended upon the ice in a long line or procession, they formed a most singular sight. If it had not been for the swiftness with which this vast retinue moved, it might have been compared to a caravan crossing the desert . . . They had all taken their whet of brandy, as usual, after divine service; and the coming of strangers among them, at this moment, adding to their hilarity, such racing commenced upon the frozen main, as reminded us of antient representations of scenes in the Circus or Hippodrome. Here were seen female charioteers contesting speed against their male companions . . .

After watching the races they headed for Vartsala. This was an experience so bad that Clarke could hardly bear to describe it, and was betrayed into a very uncharacteristic piece of chauvinism: 'It is only in viewing the state of other countries, that thy [England's] advantages can be duly estimated!'

At Vartsala, where only Finnish was spoken, they 'entered a dirty, wretched hovel, without any accommodation for travellers'.

The manners of the people were so revolting, that one hesitates in giving the description of anything so disgusting. The glasses put on the table were dirty; and this being mentioned, they attempted clean them with spittle. A woman, who entered the chamber with a saucer of butter, not only blew her nose upon her fingers, but into the palm of her hand; and then, wiping it on her petticoat, proceeded to handle all the provisions that were set forth.

The scene is reminiscent of a famous episode in Scotland, when Samuel Johnson, in similar circumstances, threw his lemonade out of the window of his inn. Clarke's determination to escape from the horrors of Vartsala led to even worse experiences:

Yet, as any thing was preferable to remaining in the wretched and unwholesome hovel where we had passed the night, we resolved to brave all the inclemency of the weather, and set out, at eight o'clock, in open sledges.

We had used every possible precaution, as to additional clothing; but it was all to no purpose.

Clarke portrays the effects of frostbite vividly – lividly, even – describing its dangers, cure, and effects.

Finally they reached the Finnish mainland, at Helsinki ('Helsing'), but finding that there was 'no place of rest and accommodation for travellers' before Turku, they put up with an obliging widowed householder at Vitikainen ('Vinkila'). Here they met a Mr Elmgreen, who was also travelling to Turku, and obligingly offered to accompany them; in fact, he continued to help them when they arrived.

From Mr Elmgreen they learned what they were already discovering for themselves:

in travelling this route, beds are a species of accommodation never found. The traveller must put together such things as he can collect; and lie down upon a table, or a few boards put together to raise him a little above the floor, which is seldom in a state for him to make his bed upon.

Clarke was the only traveller of this era who explored both northern and southern Finland, and his bad experiences of the housing, housekeeping, and standards of accommodation in the south are in striking contrast to those he had, by and large, enjoyed in Lapland and Ostrobothnia. He describes calling at a clergyman's house near Himoinen in the hope of finding accommodation, 'but the scene of wretchedness and dirt within his mansion was such, that we never even hinted at the cause of our visit'.

They reached Turku on the evening of 3 January:

On our entering this Town and University, the first thing that struck us was the unusual sound of bells, upon all the horses drawing sledges about the streets. The inhabitants pay their visits attended by this kind of music.

This was a suitably soothing end to their purgatorial passage from Stockholm.

*

The range of Clarke's knowledge, the sharpness of his observation, and the lucidity of his writing make his descriptions of Finland outstanding. The extracts given here do not reflect the geological, topographical and botanical detail which occupies much of his account. His abilities are especially evident in his descriptions of Turku. He visited the town not simply as a traveller, but as one seriously interested in the state of learning, especially of scientific learning, in this distant land. His admiration for the university and for the scholars he met is in great contrast to Wraxall's contemptuous dismissal, and is by far the most informed account by an Englishman of the state of learning in Finland, and of the only Finnish university.

After surviving the hardships and mortal dangers of the journey across the archipelago, Clarke and Cripps came close to death in their comfortable and spacious inn in Turku. They ordered fires to be lit in the two stoves in their room, but made the near-fatal mistake of closing the chimney shutter too soon, before the wood was completely burned:

The author first felt the attack: it came on with great coldness in the extremities, and a tendency to sneeze; followed by a general sensation of shivering over the whole body, and violent head-ache. Presently, he fell senseless to the floor. His companion, being roused by the noise, and finding him in this situation, attempted to raise him; but was by this time similarly affected, and had barely strength enough to call in the servants, who alarmed the people of the house. . ... Their mode of treating people under these attacks is, to carry them out naked into the open air, and rub their bodies with snow until the vital functions are restored. We felt the bad effects of this accident in violent head-ache, which lasted during many days afterwards.

Clarke does not state that he and Cripps were actually restored by these means, but it is certainly implied.

As it was probable that our stay in this place would be of some duration – both on account of our being obliged to wait for the arrival of our carriage, and also from our curiosity to make ourselves well acquainted with the university of *Åbo*, its Professors, discipline, and state of science – we sent our interpreter, the day after our arrival, to hire lodgings; and were soon provided with a very neat set of apartments, having three rooms *en suite*, besides accommodation for the servants, at the price of two rix-dollars, or four shillings *English*, per day including fire and candles. Accordingly we moved from our inn; and had scarcely taken up our abode in these comfortable chambers, when we received a visit from our former companion, Mr. *Elmgreen;* who told us that the different Professors, to whom we had letters of recommendation, were at their houses, and would be very glad to see us, and to shew us every attention in their power. This kind message convinced us that we were still within the limits of *Swedish* hospitality: and we set out to pay our respects to all of them; beginning with the celebrated Poet of *Sweden* and *Finland*, Professor *Francis Michaël Frantzën*, . . . Professor of

History and the Belles Lettres. We had before seen him at *Gamla Carleby,* during our journey in the North of *Finland,* when he was in search of a wife, as we have before mentioned. Upon the occasion of our present visit, we found him in his little study, surrounded by his books; among which, to our surprise, we observed *Addison's* Spectator, the works of our poet *Gray, Cowper's* Poems, and several other of our *English* Poets, all in their original language. Observing that we noticed his collection of *English* Authors, he said, 'We *Scandinavians* are able to appreciate the beauties of *English* literature, because the thoughts and feeling of your writers are so nearly akin to our own.'

Next on their visiting list was Henry Gabriel Porthan, 'the most learned scholar in the University'; this was the first of several meetings:

The fate of such a scholar as *Porthan* is greatly to be regretted by the literary world; because, being a native of *Finland,* and deeply versed in all that related to its history and antiquities, and himself an accomplished scholar, well read in other branches of history and antiquities, he possessed the ability, if he had possessed the means, of giving information to the world upon a subject of all others the least known; namely, the origin of the *Finlanders* and *Laplanders.* He spoke the *Latin* language, as if it had been his mother-tongue; but with that peculiarity of pronunciation belonging to all foreigners, and with a degree of volubility which rendered it sometimes difficult to apprehend exactly his meaning. The few facts which were gathered from him, during the frequent conversations we had with him, will of course be stated; but, from the little we thus gained, we could only be convinced of the extent of the loss sustained by the literary world, in not having better means of appreciating his various acquirements. *Åbo,* interdicted from all communication with *Petersburg,* and having little intercourse even with *Stockholm,* owing to the peculiar circumstances of its situation, cannot be considered as a favourable spot for the interests of literature; yet such has been the merits of its Professors, that some of them, to whom we shall presently allude, have caused their names, in spite of every obstacle, to be heard in the more-favoured walks of science.

In a letter written at this time to his friend Otter, long since returned to England, Clarke described his situation:

> I am become a student here; and I do assure you, little as I have hitherto esteemed study in a foreign university, I shall ever acknowledge my obligation to this. We have received great kindness from all the professors; but the venerable Porthan, whose *History of Finland* will render his name famous throughout Europe, is my master . . . I am become of the number of his pupils.

Clarke (and, presumably, Cripps) spent 'whole evenings conversing with him', learning about the history of Finland, and the history and nature of the Finnish language. Clarke transcribes examples of Finnish poetry, giving a 'Native song of a Finnish Maiden' in Finnish with a literal translation. On the evidence of these pages, he appears to have been a very attentive student.

Clarke gives a very exact account both of the town and of the academic structure of the university, with many details of the principal holdings in the library. The professor of chemistry, John Gadolin, 'had the kindness to show us the collection of *Minerals* belonging to the University', but despite Clarke's esteem for his attempts at improvement, it remained for him 'a wretched heap of trash'. By contrast, he had a high opinion of the botanical collections, under the care of Professor Hellenius, and he found the botanic garden 'in the highest state of cultivation'. 'A visit to this garden is sufficient to show the lovers of *botany* what may be accomplished by economy and talents', he concluded. Clarke considered the university to be superior in almost every respect to Uppsala: there 'science was a subject of conversation; at Åbo it was a subject of real and industrious research'. He considered 'the state of public morals' in the Finnish university to be superior, as well.

They attended divine service at the cathedral, and were puzzled to find themselves being laughed at by the congregation. They eventually realised that they had seated themselves on 'the female side of the aisle'. No other visitor to the cathedral in this era held it in such high esteem; despite his disdain for the paintings, one, of the crucifixion, 'a wretched piece of daubing', Clarke concluded that there 'is no building in all *Scandinavia* more worth seeing'.

While they were in Turku they witnessed the great annual fair to which Finns had travelled from the most distant parts of the country, so that Clarke felt that in this one town he was seeing a conspectus of the whole nation. He was astonished at the sacrifices which the Finns would make to obtain drink and tobacco:

> Of all their wants, the principal are constantly the same; viz. *tobacco* and *brandy* – drugs universally requisite, where mental resources are at a low ebb, for steeping in forgetfulness the *tædium vitæ*. The desire of obtaining them is so great among the *Finns* and *Lapps*, as to supersede almost every other necessary article of life. From what we saw of the *Finns*, it was evident that both

men and women would sooner eat their provisions raw, and even starve themselves, than be deprived of *brandy* and *tobacco*: therefore, if the price of an *iron-kettle*, for which a *Finn* has made a journey to *Åbo*, astonishing both as to its extent and difficulty, should encroach too much upon his little fund for supplying him with these articles, he will spend all he has in *brandy* and *tobacco*, and return home again without the utensil for which he came.

He was much struck by the contrast between the unruly life in the streets, and the cultured world of the merchants, 'living in a very elegant style'; 'we had invitations to balls and routs', while in the snowy streets outside 'the wildest *Finlanders* from the interior of the country' exhibited 'features of savage life'.

Clarke had observed earlier the complete absence of booksellers, and indeed of books in Ostrobothnia. 'Literature is at so low an ebb', he had written, 'that it may be doubted whether any traces of it may be said to exist north of *Åbo*'. His visits to the Turku booksellers were not much more successful:

There are three or four booksellers' shops, but they are worse than those of *Stockholm*. The owners of these shops are only to be found in attendance during one hour in the day – from eleven till twelve: and if a stranger, calling at that hour, is desirous of examining the books, he is not allowed to touch one of them. A catalogue, written in the *Swedish* language, is put into his hand, which is all he is permitted to see: and when he has been at the pains of examining the list, he finds it to consist entirely of *Swedish* publications; few of which are worthy of notice.

Other unusual customs which Clarke noticed in Turku were the ringing of church bells at funerals 'as we do in *England* at a wedding', and the publicising of robberies by someone walking through the streets beating a drum.

While Clarke and Cripps were enjoying a civilised life in Turku, their Swedish interpreter was travelling all the way back to Vårdö to fetch their carriage, the ice now being thick enough to bear it. As soon as it arrived, they took leave of their friends – there is no account of any farewell scene – and set off for St Petersburg. They travelled as quickly as possible over the 'dreary uniformity' of the snow on the road to Helsinki, the 'houses of relay' 'seldom rising to mediocrity'. Even in winter, though, he could appreciate 'a country full of picturesque beauty', where 'the whole country appears decked with farm houses and village churches'. Helsinki he describes as 'a small but handsome town':

> The houses have an appearance of comfort; and the inhabitants, we were informed, live in perfect harmony and good-will with each other. We experienced great attention and politeness from many of them. Nothing can be more gay and pleasing than the scene, exhibited on the ice, from *Helsingfors* to the fortress of *Sveaborg*, which is situate on an island, distant two *English* miles. The road is marked on the snow by trees, or large branches of the pine, planted in the ice. Sledges of all sizes and descriptions, open and covered, of business, burthen, or pleasure, plain or decorated, with beautiful little prancing *Finland* horses, are seen moving with the utmost rapidity, backwards and forwards, the whole way, from morning to night. Officers with their servants, ladies, soldiers, peasants, artificers, engineers, form a crowded *promenade*, more interesting and amusing than that of *Hyde Park* in *London*, or the *Corso* at *Rome*.

After visiting Suomenlinna they continued to Porvoo, where they 'stopped at a good but extravagant inn'. Arriving at Loviisa

> we were stopped by a Custom-house officer; who intended, as we supposed, that we should unpack all our baggage: but he at last observed, that if we would give him something, he would suffer us to pass. The manners of the people began to change; and we found nothing to remark, but dirt and drunkenness. The town is rather pretty and the principal street is wide.

No traveller of the time expressed more astonishment at 'the extreme contrast' experienced when crossing the border: '[t]he country is still *Finland,* but it is *Russian Finland*'. '[A] few miles,' Clarke wrote, 'nay, even a few yards conduct you from a land of hospitality and virtue, to a den of thieves.' Apart from petty theft, the travellers suffered from the vindictiveness of the Russian customs inspector, and the rest of the journey to St Petersburg, 'through a country more inhospitable than the deserts of *Tahtary*', provided 'a catalogue of difficulties which quickly succeeded each other'.

These volumes provide the most substantial British account of Finland during this era, yet they were little more than a prelude to Clarke's travels, which were to occupy him and Cripps for another two and a half years, taking them through Russia, Tartary, Circassia, Asia Minor, Syria, Palestine, Egypt, Turkey and Greece. In 1808 Clarke was appointed the first Professor of Mineralogy at Cambridge. He began to publish his account in 1810; it was incomplete at the time of his death in 1822, the second of the Scandinavian volumes coming out posthumously in 1823.

John Carr

Just as Clarke and Cripps were returning from their long and arduous journey a traveller of a very different sort was setting off from London for the Baltic. John Carr was what is now called a belletrist; he published verse, drama, and a number of books of travel which were characterised rather unkindly in *The Dictionary of National Biography*: 'though without much intrinsic merit, [they] obtained a wide circulation on account of their light, gossipy style, and the fact that in this species of literature there was then comparatively little competition'; his writings 'soon fell into well-deserved obscurity'. For better or for worse, Carr has a very distinct style: his poetic evocation of the idyllic scenery of the Åland archipelago certainly has no rival. The Dedication to *A Northern Summer or Travels Round the Baltic* (1805) hardly inspires any further reading:

> It was on the 14th of May, 1804, that, impelled by an ardent desire of contemplating the great and interesting volume of man, and by hope of ameliorating a state of health which has too often awakened the solicitude of maternal affection, and of friendly sympathy, the writer of these pages bade adieu to a spot in which the morning of life had rolled over his head, and which a thousand circumstances had endeared to him.

He followed what was soon to become the established route: from Harwich via Denmark to Stockholm, thence through Turku and Vyborg to St Petersburg, and home through Germany. Carr gives a description of the vessels which plied the Stockholm route before the coming of the steamers. They were

> single-masted, and resemble a shallop with a raised deck, and a pink or sharp stern, which is much lower than the fore part, and is frequently under water: they cannot live long in rough weather.

A lazier traveller than Carr it would be difficult to envisage. In the Åland archipelago the slow progress of the boat suited his languorous mood, and brought out the poet in him:

> Here we landed, and ascended the rocks, which, sparingly clothed with green moss, rose from the water's edge with the most grand, romantic and picturesque disorder. Before us the rich crimson suffusion of the sun, just sunk behind a dark undulating line of fir forests, gave at once tranquillity and tone to the lake-appearance of this arm of the Baltic, which was enlivened by the white-lagging sails of a few boats, that on the opposite side softly and slowly creeped through the deep shadows of the shores, crowned by the woods of Liston-cottage.

The following evening was striking in another way: Carr presents a pastoral idyll which must surely have owed much more to his poetic imagination than to his powers of observation:

> This island was indeed a most enchanting scene: upon its romantic summit of grey rock we found a little cottage embowered in trees of fir, ash, and elder, that might well be called 'the *peasants' nest.*' A fisherman, his aged mother, his wife and children, formed the population of this beautiful spot. A little field of grass, on which a cow

was grazing, another of corn, a garden, and the waters of the Baltic, which again resembled a lake, supplied them with all their wants, and all their riches. Here it seemed as if the heart could no longer ache, as if ambition might wish to be what he beheld, and that love might ponder on the past without a pang. The inside of the cottage was neat and cheerful; the good old lady, with the children in their shirts playing round her, sat knitting by the light of a sprightly fire, and under locks of snow presented a face at peace with all the world.

'It was', he writes, 'just such a spot as the poetical spirit of Cowper would have coveted.' English poetry of the later eighteenth century describes many such idealised pastoral scenes; the spirit of Goldsmith as well as Cowper is at work here. The idyll faded as the travellers approached the Finnish mainland, where the islands 'ceased to present any picturesque object'.

I do not think that any British traveller in Finland has ever recorded such muted enthusiasm for any place as Carr did for Turku. He admitted that the castle had 'a very picturesque appearance', and that 'many of the houses are handsome', but the cathedral displayed 'no attractions to the eye', the university was 'not in a flourishing state', and the library was 'little worthy of notice'. The only feature which caught his attention inspired some mildly energetic irony. This was the decoration of the room where he slept:

At Abo, my bed was made up in an appendage to the ball-room, and had much of Finnish decoration to recommend it. The walls were laboriously painted in glowing colours, with flaming swords, fiddles, and flutes, and seraphim's heads, which were saved from the voracious and expanded beaks of griffins, by the

99

tender interposition of baskets of flowers, and over the whole there was a pretty sprinkling of sphinxes and the royal arms of Sweden.

Carr's principal concern in Finland was to travel as fast as possible. It was now mid-July, and the flies 'annoyed us beyond imagination'. He describes a miserable night spent at the post-house at Mjölbolsta, near Karjaa; of all the post-houses on the Great Coastal Road, this was the one most frequently execrated by travellers:

> The sides of the room were completely encrusted with flies, who at this moment were recruiting themselves for the mischief of the next day; and mice and tarrakans, or beetles, shared the possession of the floor. In two corners of this dolorous hole stood two cribs, each furnished with a bed of straw, a bronze-coloured blanket well charged with fleas, and a greasy coverlid.

The flies 'besieged us in battalions'; Carr describes the humiliating failure of an attempted counter-attack on them.

The next day they passed by several forest fires, caused by farmers clearing the land; one 'at some distance', 'had a very sublime and novel effect'. Apart from passing references to Porvoo and Loviisa, Carr's next description is of the bridge over the Kymijoki. Of the many travellers who mention this little landmark it is Carr who gives the most readable account:

> About three miles from Louisa, another garrison town, we reached the frontiers of Sweden, and in a custom and guard house beheld the last remains of that country. A Swedish soldier raised the cross bar, such as I described in Denmark; we passed over a bridge which crosses a branch of the river Kymen, and divides

Sweden from Russia. The exclusive right of painting this little bridge had very nearly inflamed these rival nations to the renewal of all those horrors, which have so long and so prodigally wasted the blood and treasure of both countries . . . This marvellous dispute, after a stormy discussion, with the sword half-drawn, was settled in the following manner, viz Sweden was to use what size brush and what colours she preferred, upon one half of the bridge, and on the other Russia the like materials in the way that best suited her fancy.

As he got closer to St Petersburg, Carr seemed to become more cheerful, and in this mood approached Hamina:

We now began to reckon our stations by versts: a verst is about three quarters of an English mile, and is marked upon a post, painted like the bridge, somewhat resembling, only that the verst-post is square and much taller, a barber's pole. The rapidity of our travelling, and the frequent appearance of these memorials of our velocity, were the only cheering circumstances that we met with. Upon the road we saw several peasants bareheaded, cropped, fair, with shorn beards, and booted. We met with little or no delay for horses: the peasant, to whom they belonged, attended us to take them back. After passing through a country the most wretched and rocky imaginable, a country formerly wrested by the Russians from the Swedes, in which the gloomy sterility of nature was only once relieved by the waterfalls which attracted our notice at Hagfors, and a large camp of several Russian regiments, who had a very fine appearance, we reached, at eleven o'clock at night, the draw-bridge of Fredricksham, the gates of which had been some time closed. After repeatedly knocking, a little beardless officer presented himself, and very politely requested to have our passports and post-order, with which he disappeared. Here we waited in suspense for three quarters of an hour: all owing to the provoking integrity and detention of the custom-house officer at the barrier. At length we halted before a house, which our little officer, as well as we could understand him, informed us was the only inn in the town. Here we found no person moving: after trying at the door for some time in vain, I peeped into the front room, and beheld a spectacle *à la mode de Russe,* to me completely novel; it was a collection of nine or ten men and women all lying, with their clothes on, promiscuously upon the floor, like pigs, heads and tails together. An officer passing by informed us that this was a private house, and that the inn, in Russ called a kabac, was the next door; but that it was locked up and empty, the host having gone to enjoy the breezes of the sea for a few days. This circumstance plainly demonstrated one of two things; either that this part of Russia is not much frequented by travellers, or, as I frequently experienced, that an inn-keeper, however poor, is very indifferent whether he affords them any accommodation.

We had been travelling all day under a fervid sun, were covered with dust, and parched with thirst; our Abo ham was glowing to the bone, our last bottle of claret was as warm as milk from the cow, and our poor exhausted horses were licking the walls of an adjoining building to cool their tongues. In this dilemma I beheld an elegant young officer, uncovered, in a dark bottle-green uniform (the legionary colour of Russia), and an elderly gentleman, upon whose breast two resplendent stars shone, coming towards us: these stars were two propitious constellations. The principal personage addressed us in a very kind and conciliatory manner in French. Upon our explaining our situation, he said, 'I am very sorry this fellow is out of the way, but it shall make no difference. When Englishmen enter Russia it is to experience hospitality, not inconvenience; trust to me, I will immediately provide for you:' he bowed, gave directions to an officer who followed at a distance, and passed on. This amiable man proved to be the Count Meriandoff, the Governor of Russian Finland, who, fortunately for us, had arrived about an hour before from Wyborg. An officer soon afterwards came to us, and conducted us to a very handsome house belonging to a Russian gentleman of fortune. Our kind host, who spoke a little English, introduced us into a spacious drawing-room, where we went to rest upon two delightful beds, which were mounted upon chairs. Our poor servant, after the manner of the Russians, ranked no higher in our host's estimation than a faithful mastiff, and was left to make a bed of our great coats on the floor of the entry, and to sleep *comme il plait à Dieu.*

After this glimpse of civilised living, Carr's final view of Finland, before arriving at Vyborg, provoked his most powerful piece of description, an extraordinary contrast to the idyllic picture he gave of the scenery and inhabitants of the Åland archipelago:

We halted at a village of old crazy hovels, composed of trunks of trees, rudely thrown across each other, and perched upon granite rocks; every one of these forlorn abodes was out of the perpendicular, whilst, from a little hole which feebly admitted the light, the smoke issued. The inhabitants were nearly naked, and looked like a race of animals formed in the anger of heaven. Instead of the green refreshing blade, parched hoary moss covered the earth; where the limpid brook ought to have rippled, a narrow, slimy, brown stream, of reeking offensive water, crawled indolently and unwholesomely along. Not a tree was to be seen; not even a melancholy fir. Time, that bids the barrenness of nature bear, that enabled the shepherd and his flock to find shelter and rich pasture in the altered desert, has passed over these regions without shedding his accustomed beneficence. These people, or, as they are called, the Finns, I found always distinguishable in the capital from the proper Russian, by their squalid and loathsome appearance.

Carr's final experience before arriving at Vyborg was at the post-house at Terijoki, where the postmaster 'having given me to understand that I might use the bed after he had done with it, very composedly jumped into it with his clothes on'.

Sir Robert Ker Porter

Robert Ker Porter was a painter of considerable repute in his time. He grew up in Edinburgh, and as a boy became fascinated by paintings of battles. After moving to London he became an academy student at Somerset House at the age of about fourteen, studying under Benjamin West. He soon began to be known for his historical landscapes, for his abilities as a theatrical scene painter, and also as a portrait painter. During his career he exhibited thirty-eight pictures at the Royal Academy. In 1804 he was appointed 'historical painter' to Czar Alexander I, a post which has been described as one 'which belonged to the quasi-scientific, quasi-romantic spirit of the age'. He lived in St Petersburg for more than three years, becoming engaged to a Russian princess, Mary von Scherbatoff. He was forced to abandon his courtship abruptly when the Russian alliance with Napoleon made him, as an Englishman, *persona non grata*. This is what took him on his journey through Finland to Stockholm in December 1807. Here he was received at court, and was later (1806) knighted by King Gustav IV Adolf.

His *Travelling Sketches in Russia and Sweden During the Years 1805, 1806, 1807, 1808* (1809) was published in two sumptuous volumes, weighing in at more than two kilos. It contains forty-one full-page plates, all by himself, but the interest of his book is rather in contrast to its size; a biographer wrote that it displays 'neither remarkable literary faculty nor any special powers of observation'. I think that the extracts which follow show this judgement to be a little harsh. Porter shows at times a painter's eye, both for scenery and for the the appearance and dress of the local population. His journey through Finland occupies about thirty pages of his text, and his descriptions are indeed not much more than sketches. This was because his only concern was to get to Stockholm as quickly as possible; his descriptions are found mainly in the account of his hazardous journey from Turku through the archipelago, when he was stranded for days at a time on several occasions. He gives a very limited account of his overland journey, except to complain about the inns: in Vyborg he writes of 'all manner of filthy abominations'.

The recurring refrain is the uncouthness of the natives; a favourite epithet is 'frightful'. His illustration of *A Finn* was so striking that he felt obliged to justify its accuracy:

> The Finlanders are of a small stature, sharp featured, and usually without any apparent beard. They have light complexions; with fair hair, worn long and *uncombed* on each side of their head. Brown woollen kaftans short to the knee; with loose black pantaloons and boots, make up their apparel. Now and then, as a wonderful finery, a sort of worked decoration adorns their upper garments. Their caps are unvaryingly of the same shape. In short, seeing one Finlander is seeing them all; and my sketch is as like their rude exterior as if it had been cut out by one of their own taylors. A most barbarous animal you will think I have made the poor Fin.

Perhaps for us now the main interest in Porter's account is his awareness of the political situation, and the details he gives of the military activities – 'numerous regiments . . . cannon, war carriages' – on the Russian side of the border:

> Thirty thousand men, I am told, is the present Russian force in [Russian] Finland. And to me it will be surprising, if they do not fall upon Sweden much sooner than

that kingdom expects the attack . . . [At the frontier] I found a very slender guard; and after the usual formalities, passed through them with great ease. I was rather surprised to find so slight a defence opposed to the coming enemy; but as I proceeded my astonishment increased, as I rarely saw any thing bearing the least affinity to arms: and when I recalled the large army I had just quitted, on the full march to overwhelm this country, I was totally at a loss how to account for so unguarded a security.

The contrast of the large-scale military build-up in Russia with the trusting peacefulness of the Finnish countryside just a few miles away both astonished and worried him:

Whatever may be the occult reason for the present tranquillity, all is at perfect rest in Swedish Finland. Liberty and comfort smile every where; peace sits on every countenance, and decorates the landscape, as if this had been her chosen reign for many a year. The view was delightful; and had I not been sure that Bellona was at my heels, ready to burn up their present and promised happiness, I might have enjoyed the scene; but the prospect of its impending destruction, like the *mystical lore* of the Scottish wizard, disturbed my fancy; and I was glad to press forward.

Porter was showing remarkable prescience here. He was, in fact, the last traveller to record crossing into 'Swedish Finland', since in the following year the Peace of Hamina ceded all of Finland to Russia.

The speed of travelling was what now impressed him; the horses were fast – 'their motion in descending the hills is so swift, as to be really terrific' – and were so readily available at every posting stage that he seems hardly to have stopped.

This, presumably is why he was unable to 'pass any encomiums on the towns and villages I travelled through in my way to Abo'. He did at least manage to notice that the population on the Swedish side were no longer savages; their faces resembled 'the lower class of Germans; and their manners are good natured'. The fences he thought similar to those of northern America, and the landscape towards the end of the journey 'strongly resembles the north of Ireland'. It is surprising to find an artist noticing so little.

He saw 'all worthy observation at Abo'. The 'all' consisted of the university and the 'church' (as he called the cathedral), or more specifically the organ, which 'may be ranked above the best in Europe; its tones indeed equalled any I had ever heard'. The university, he wrote, 'is admirable; and the new edifice for the use of the students is in great forwardness, and seems to promise both convenience and beauty.'

Porter imagined with charming naivety the speed and ease which the journey to Sweden would have offered in summer, lasting 'no longer than from fourteen to twenty four hours':

> gliding gently over the waves, the happy he who travels under summer suns, avoids the inconveniences of stoppages, the expensive wretchedness of the islands, and lands himself fresh and gay on the opposite shore.

He glamorised his expectations a little, following the pattern of several other travellers of the time by dressing up his journey in classical garb. In the conclusion of his letter from Turku (his book is cast as letters to a friend) he wrote:

> I am told that Ulysses never met with more horrible perils amongst the isles of the Syrens, than I am to encounter among the isles of Bothnia. I fear that they will be in less agreeable shapes than beautiful women;

and expecting rather to meet with sea storms than sea nymphs, I commit myself to your orisons; hoping soon, from Stockholm, again to sign myself your faithful friend.

It was not to be. The next letter is not from Stockholm but from Vartsala, 'the very *acmé* of northern discomfort', recording a journey which could hardly have been less agreeable.

Porter and his 'honest servant Gerard Schmidt' (who seems to have been a companion as well as a servant, sharing accommodation and meals, and even accompanying him to church), 'sallied forth in [their] kibitkas towards Elsing, a village about six Swedish miles from Abo'. The problem at this time of year was that the ice was too thick for the boats but too weak for their sledges, on which the kibitkas were fastened. Believing optimistically that 'an intermingled fluid and frozen mode of conveyance might be possible', they set off, 'escorted and assisted' by 'a number of villagers of both sexes'. After a perilous journey – 'a cold, wet and benumbing perambulation' – the villagers finally got them ashore on Vartsala. Instead of the 'warm comforts' which he had been anticipating

such chilling wretchedness, such dirt and penury were exhibited here, that I had much ado to persuade myself not to prefer returning to the dangers of the gulf, before passing a night in so miserable a spot.

If the bed was bad, the board was worse: '[t]he wherewithal to satisfy hunger, is simple and circumscribed; viz. black bread, with a most nauseous beer, and, by way of luxury, a little bad salt fish'. Like most travellers of this time, Porter had learnt the necessity on such journeys of being 'provided with every thing in the provision way' and had brought his own food and drink with him. If he had not, he would have had to keep going with just the 'Spartan bread'. After eight days, and with both his provisions and his patience running out, Porter decided to make a break for it, despite the warnings of the 'rascally old postmaster' whom Porter suspected of prolonging their captivity for his own profit. By giving the peasants 'a very handsome price for their assistance' he managed to set off, but eventually 'got into a labyrinth of ice shoals and impediments of every kind' and was obliged to return to Vartsala in the middle of the following night, 'wet, benumbed, and sulky'.

A hard frost prompted a second bid for freedom, but when they reached open water it began to freeze around them; the peasant guides insisted on returning before it was too late, and the travellers, humiliated again, returned to Vartsala at four the next morning.

After four or five more days on the island Porter was expressing himself ready 'to think of turning Robinson Crusoe at once, and, with my faithful Friday, scooping myself out a decent dwelling in one of the rocks', when a group of travellers from Kumlinge arrived. '"The water which brings will take," said my sagacious attendant', so the next day they bade a final adieu to Wartsala. It may have been third time lucky, but it was certainly not plain sailing, as they 'met accumulations of mishaps, dangers, and long cold wadings over the bending ice':

> I was wet through, and so frozen, that had it not been for the warm tobacco pipe I constantly kept in my mouth (this disagreeable custom is absolutely necessary here), I believe I should have expired with the piercing cold.

After finally embarking they had a strong gale and floating ice to contend with. They experienced 'many complete duckings' and lost some of their luggage before landing on Avå.

After the horrors on Wartsala, Porter's description of Avå verges on the fulsome; 'our reception was primitively kind,' he wrote 'and might have graced a city':

> The wives and daughters of the boatmen ran out towards us, and approaching myself and Schmidt with the same cordiality, invited us in, and spread their tables with a collection of eatables. To be sure their abodes were mere hovels; yet the hospitality and benevolence which reigned within, and the content which sat smiling on their honest countenances, gave a charm to everything around. We forgot our mishaps; and partaking, not only of their simple fare, but of the amusements they presented to divert us, the whole place in a few minutes became a scene of the most innocent gaiety.

This is another idealised pastoral scene, a winter version of Carr's summer idyll a few years earlier. Their landlord ('another good soul') 'had a very pretty wife', and produced a violin to get the dancing going. 'A general ball then ensued: and really I never saw a set of people more delighted.'

Porter compares the primitive music and dancing ('the barbarity in their leaping gesticulations') of the islanders very unfavourably to that of the Russians, whose social manners 'bespeak a people far advanced in the refinements of taste'. The personal appearance of the Ålanders, though, was quite a different matter: 'The men here are well looking and the women extremely handsome,' he writes, bringing his portrait-painter's eye to bear on them. 'Indeed, independent of their fair and ruddy complexions, the ingenuousness of their countenances, gives the finishing touch of beauty.'

Such was Porter's hurry to get to Stockholm that he did

not consider staying longer than necessary even on this idyllic island, but set off at eight o'clock the following morning, arriving six hours later at Torsholma, 'even so early, being obliged to take up our quarters for the night'. Immediately on landing he saw the church, and here it is the eye of the landscapist rather than of the portraitist that is brought into play:

> The structure is simple and picturesque. Not many yards from it, on a rising ground, stands a high tower of a similar colour, wherein are the bells. This religious edifice is very romantically situated, being on the edge of a small lake, and boldly surrounded by vast masses of finely diversified rock. Not a tree or a shrub is perceptible on even the most sheltered spots; and therefore the beauty of these views consists wholly in the outline and broad sweeps of colouring

Despite '[h]aving received civilities from the natives, similar to those of Arvo' they set off early the next day, having 'bid the good folks adieu'. They arrived eighteen hours later in Kumlinge, greeted by a 'multitude of wind mills'. At the post house – 'tolerably comfortable' – he enjoyed 'a measureless dinner' of two fine black woodcock. They set off the next morning, but were driven back by storms, which continued to prevent their departure for several days more. 'Having nothing better to do', he and a fellow traveller explored the island, and calling at the parsonage were surprised to find that the parson was hospitable, lively, and intelligent:

> If I may judge of all Swedish pastors from the present specimen, they live in clover. All was smiling around our host, who set before us cold hams and fowls sufficient to satisfy two famishing wolves, had they stopped at his

door. He spoke a little German; by which good fortune we gained more information in ten minutes, than we could gather in as many hours from the pantomimic converse to which we had lately been reduced.

Conversing in German, he found out a good deal about the church and the parish, and was impressed with the commendable 'industry of the Kumlingers': the minister's 'account of this little hive of human bees was truly gratifying'. Inside the church he viewed the adornments with a professional's eye, but what he saw was a little outside his usual terms of reference as an artist:

The interior of the building is curiously adorned in a most Gothic taste, but by no means badly executed. It is painted in compartments, with pictures representing the life of Christ; with this small difference from what it ought to be, that the designs would better fit a legend of heathen gods, than a representation of the gospel. The roof has not escaped the labour of this indefatigable artist: angels, saints, and odd animals, like nothing on earth or in the seas, are swarming about the ceiling; and seem like a flight of locusts looking down on whom they may devour.

On the Sunday they attended the minister to church, and Porter was impressed by the sermon, although he did not understand a word. 'My companion and myself returned to our inn, much pleased with our rustic preacher's eloquence, of look and action!'

Finally, after a 'few monotonous melancholy days' and two failed attempts to leave Kumlinge, a favourable wind took them, in three hours, to Vargata. As they crossed the island by horse 'the beauty of the country, the rich woods and luxuriant copses, made so striking a contrast to the naked spot I had just quitted, that I could hardly believe my-self awake'. They continued to Skarpans; even on the short crossing to Åland and from there he endured three immersions and fulminated against 'the ever varying wretchedness of these horrible isles'. They crossed by post to Eckerö, from where they were finally to take the boat to Grisslehamn. It was, he reflected, exactly one month since he had left St Petersburg. Porter's account of the inn where he stayed at Eckerö is a classic of its kind, and reads like a parody of the sort of response that upper-class Englishmen sometimes think is expected of them abroad:

> The inn, house, hotel, with whatever title you choose to honour it, had as much pretensions to the one name as to another, all were equally unfitting; and when I drew towards it, I fancied that my servant had made a mistake, and was ushering me into a cow shed. All the other execrable habitations I had visited; even the den of Warsala itself, were palaces to this. Filth greeted my eyes and nose at the first step: the salute was too potent to be borne, and turning about, I told my followers that if I herded with wolves, I would not enter so murderous a hole. However *necessitas non habet leges*; I could not get a boat to convey me onward till the next morning; and so I was obliged to cover my plumes, and pass the *thirtieth day* of my watery pilgrimage under this anath-ematised roof.

The elements still had not finished with him. 'The demon of frustration again put his hand between me and the wished-for haven', and he was forced to put up on Signildsskär, 'to seek shelter among desolation and horrors'. This he described as a 'naked rock', which was 'as bare of fertility as its few inhabitants are of honesty; bleak as may be their situation, their hospitality is bleaker'. His 'old extortionate host' told Porter how, in summer, his three cattle swam long distances from island to island in search of grass:

> I forgot to ask my informer, whether the damsels of his household did not sometimes, in the European fashion, take a trip to the other isles on the backs of these adventurous animals. It would be no very uninteresting sight, to see one or two of the pretty Swedish girls, with their fair hair floating in the wind, speeding their way through the summer waves to their expecting lovers on a distant shore. Could I have found cow or calf inclined to brave the element in winter, I believe I would have tried my luck, and galloped, *à la Neptune*, through the waters, to the fair haven of Grisslehamn.

After two days in this 'purgatory', 'a fine morning appeared, with a following wind', and Porter, leaping into his boat as if he were Achilles being 'translated to the upper world again', finally set sail for the Swedish mainland

Love conquered Porter's dislike of northern travel. In 1811 he revisited Russia and in the following year married his Russian princess. He made further travels before being appointed British consul in Venezuela, and being knighted in 1813. His chief fame today is as a 'remarkable pioneer in Near Eastern archaeology'. He lived fifteen years in Caracas, returned to England in 1841, and travelled again to St Petersburg, where he died and was buried in the following year.

John Thomas James

Porter was a reluctant traveller through Finland, and his account reflects the fact. John Thomas James went for much more positive reasons: he was a Student (that is, a college fellow) of Christ Church, Oxford, and travelled with two companions, Sir James Riddell and W. MacMichael, 'M.B. Radcliffe Travelling Fellow of the University of Oxford', to make scientific and industrial observations. His *Journal of a Tour in Germany, Sweden, Russia, Poland during the Years 1813 and 1814* was published in 1816, and quickly went into second and third editions. Other European journeys followed, and led to James publishing well-regarded studies of Italian and northern European painting. After taking holy orders he was appointed Bishop of Calcutta, in succession to Reginald Heber, but died in India after less than two years.

The three travellers followed what was now the established route from Stockholm to St Petersburg, setting out in late February, 1813, over the ice. James's book is the first record of travelling in the Grand Duchy of Finland, and he duly records entering Russia, with all the customs formalities, at Eckerö:

> The island scenery appeared, as we journeyed, even at this time, beautiful; the dark lush of the fir formed a strong contrast with the silvery fleeces of snow that roofed the forest, and the whole seemed to have assumed a new charm in this livery of winter.

It took them only four days to reach Turku, a straightforward journey, and very different from Clarke's or Porter's:

our road was an undeviating line from place to place, no obstacle presented itself: we passed over the fields, through the woods, across the ice; hill and dale, land and water, were all alike.

The only scientific or industrial observation he recorded in Finland was made here in among the islands:

So little was the division of labour studied, or the appropriation of means, that we observed the corn-mills almost equalled in number the houses of the villages.

The following passage throws some light on their travelling habits:

For our own subsistence, it was absolutely necessary to carry with us our provisions: coffee was the only article of luxury which they had hoarded up for the use of a chance traveller. We cut off our meat and bread, as occasion required, from our store with a cleaver or hatchet, and having been dressed at Stockholm before we set out, the beef steaks, etc. were unfrozen by the application of cold water, then placed for a few minutes in the stove-oven, and served up to table as if fresh from the hand of the cook. Our wine and brandy underwent a partial decomposition, and the watery particles were converted to a core of ice.

James and his companions 'thought a halt for a short time might not be ill requited' in Turku, 'the great university of Finland'. He gives a brief account of the new regime in Finland, a few pages about the history of the university, and a plodding description of the cathedral, but says nothing of where he stayed or who he met. His description of the new university buildings is much more detailed than anything given by other travellers of the period:

the buildings of the college have been lately renewed at the expense of the present Emperor of Russia; nor was his generosity confined to the act of giving alone, but, with a truly liberal spirit, he has deigned to follow the plan that was intended to have been put into execution by Gustavus IV. It is a plain edifice constructed with the red granite of the country, containing the several lecture-rooms, a library, a consistory, and a hall for state occasions; the last in an unfinished state but showing great promise of magnificence. It is adorned with some beautiful columns of polished granite and (as we particularly remarked) with the bust of its intentional, as well as its real benefactor. There were also six *bas reliefs* in compartments on the wall, executed by a pupil of Sergel, and neither deficient in taste or spirit: their subjects were illustrative of the history of learning in these parts, and commenced with a fable from the Edda of the miracles of Vienamunda, the Finnish Orpheus, who taught the bears (the undoubted aborigines) to dance to the sound of his oaten pipe: the series finished with a representation in prospect of the ceremonies which were yet to take place on the solemn inauguration of the Emperor Alexander.

He describes attending divine service, which, he discovered, did not end with the clergyman's concluding prayers:

His succeeding catalogue somewhat surprised us: he recounted the sales of houses made, or about to be made, then added the direction of the unclaimed letters now lying at the post-office, with some other notices of a similar description . . . I must add in compliment to the piety of the Fins, that certainly no other mode of publication would have given these matters an equal chance of notoriety.

Although he does not record any conversations, he felt confident enough to give his opinion of the new regime in Finland: 'I do not know that the late annexation to the Russian dominions has been productive of any symptoms of discontent or ill-will'. He considered that Finland would now enjoy greater stability under the protection of a major power, and noted that taxes collected in Finland were, to use the modern term, hypothecated for Finnish use. His views were shared by most of the travellers who ventured any opinion at all on the political state of Finland after 1809.

In Helsinki, two days later, they had barely settled in their hotel when they were disturbed by the sound of a church bell and a drum, which they were told was the way of announcing a fire. They joined the crowd which 'was assembling from all quarters' and headed over the ice to Suomenlinna:

> The building was in a short time consumed to ashes: little other mischief, however, ensued; although it would be impossible to compliment very highly the skill of those engaged in extinguishing the fire. Though they were militia men, and of course inured to some notions of the advantages of regularity and order, it was with great difficulty that we were able to induce them to form a line for the sake of passing the buckets in succession; they seemed highly delighted, however, when this was done, and grinned upon us in gratitude.

'A sight of this nature', he concluded 'is never devoid of certain features of grandeur and sublimity.' The light of the fire seen over the frozen sea 'was a sight which no lapse of time will ever efface from my recollection'. James's expertise in fire-fighting is perhaps explained by the fact that while

at Oxford he had assisted in fighting a fire which destroyed
his college rooms, together with all his property, at Christ
Church.

The travellers enjoyed the winter scenery, and the following day walked around the Suomenlinna fortress, which
James described at length, with a lot of technical detail:

> After our walk we had the pleasure of dining with
> the hospitable admiral, who spoke English extremely
> well . . . Dinner concluded, we sallied forth again, and
> partook for the first time, of the amenities of the ice-
> hill, the merry-go-round, etc. and what was still more
> diverting, made a trip over the sea with a vessel moving
> with skaits upon the ice . . . Her motion was tremen-
> dously rapid, and she held a complement of twenty or
> thirty persons: but as the snow was necessarily cleared
> out for her track, the length of her voyage was of lim-
> ited extent; the circuit was ingeniously enough carried
> in the form of a pentagon, so as to enable her to take
> advantage of every wind.

They finished their evening 'at the little theatre in Helsingfors, and at night resumed [their] journey'.

James seems to have enjoyed some civilised diversions in
Helsinki, but he had really no curiosity about the country
through which he was travelling. Nonetheless he offers his
readers an example of the sort of general characterisation of
a foreign race that British travellers of all eras seem prone to
make, and to regard as sufficient comment:

> Upon a general view of their condition, these people
> are not much improved (the rustics at least) since the
> days when we first hear their names mentioned; and
> the short pithy description of Tacitus is often quoted in
> allusion to their present habits and character. It would

be unfair to expect much of such a nation, considering that in addition to the incapacitating rigour of their climate, they have, for a great part of the intervening ages, laboured under the subjection of their more powerful neighbours.

The journey to Vyborg was one of 'uninterrupted solitude'. Crossing the bridge 'that once marked the point of separation between Swedish and Russian Finland' was the only landmark that he noted – now only an historic one.

George Green

What may be regarded as the first travel guide for travellers to 'Russian Finland' was published in 1813 with the misleading title *An Original Journal from London to St. Petersburgh, by Way of Sweden*. The author was George Green, an English merchant who lived in Russia between 1805 and 1807. In his Preface Green makes the intentions of the book clear:

> [T]he Author, besides describing the public buildings, such as palaces, statues, bridges, towns, &c. &c. has been careful to insert that kind of local information which a writer, anxious to rank as eminent, might deem unworthy of his notice.

Green's jumbled list of sights shows a hint of contempt that, as a merchant, he feels for writers who, 'striving for literary eminence', felt that they were above concerning themselves with the practicalities of travel. He insists that his book is 'written by a real Traveller, from observations on the spot, and published with the view of conveying useful information'. The information about St Petersburg includes the sorts of detail which a modern traveller would expect to find in a guide: information about post offices, coach fares, weights and measures, average temperatures, and churches. There is also an English-Russian vocabulary section. Confident and informed though he sounds, he does not seem to have known that Finland had ceased to belong to Sweden four years before his book was published! None of his detailed advice about Customs regulations, currency and exchange rates would have been of any use at all to his readers for this particular part of their journey.

Despite its title, the book is not cast as a journal; the Finland pages give brief information about each of the main stopping places on the route from Hamina to Stockholm. The information is mainly practical and financial ('The best person to address for this exchange of money here [Hamina] is a Mr. Bran'), but Green occasionally allows himself a more descriptive comment, as the following sequence shows:

SWEDEN

LOUISA

Is an open town upon a bay of the Gulph of Finland; here is the first Swedish garrison, and your Swedish passport and baggage are here examined. You will perceive a visible change between Russian and Swedish Finland; in the first, the houses have more the appearance of sepulchres than the habitations of human beings, as they are only one story high, built with large trees piled and mortized one upon another; being without chimnies, the smoke, as it issues from the gabel end, colours them black as ink, and very few of them are glazed. But the village houses in Swedish Finland are much more decent, being boarded on the outsides; besides they all have chimnies and glazed windows, and are most of them painted a dark red colour.

BERGO

Is a tolerably good town, with a decent inn, where you may get supper, a bed, wine, and coffee for breakfast, for three dollars and sixteen schellings.

WELLIOSEI

A bad post, restive horses, and drunken drivers.

HELSINGFORTH

A large town, with a great home and foreign trade. Here is a tolerable inn, where the landlady speaks English.

Green was at one with contemporary travellers in his description of a typical post-house:

> To enter one of these post-house kitchens, will excite a sigh to see the misery and filth it contains: it is generally a large room, with several beds and a stove in it; the ceiling is loaded with hundreds of small black cakes, baked in the month of October, and, having a hole in the middle, they are put upon a stick, and in this manner hung up. These poor wretches have nothing to light them of an evening but a few thin split pieces of fir, stuck in the wall, or carried about in their hands from place to place. The post-houses use no candles, but they keep very small ones for travellers.

In Turku he recommends 'a convenient inn, at the sign of *Le Victoire;* the accommodations are good, and the landlord an intelligent man'. He gives a slightly sinister warning about the crossing to Wartsala, one which Porter would have benefited from:

> before the waters are sufficiently frozen to bear the horses and carriage, and too much for the passage of the boats, you are left at the mercy of the inhabitants.

Lastly, his brief comments on Vartsala itself are both striking and rather curiously phrased:

> The inhabitants are almost amphibious, but very harmless and stupid, except where their interest is concerned, but though they will impose, they will never rob you.

The females of this island have a singular mode of dressing their hair.

One can see from these extracts that Green was making no attempt at literary eminence; his rather idiosyncratic, scatter-gun approach to his subject, added to his problems with English syntax, are nonetheless an effective medium for providing 'useful information'. His list of stopping places between Turku and Grisslehamn, and the distances between them, is given in Appendix 3.

Robert Pinkerton

Robert Pinkerton was a Scottish agent of the British and Foreign Bible Society, who late in his life put together an account of Russia 'compiled from notes made on the spot, during travels, at different times'. This was published in 1833 as *Russia: or, Miscellaneous Observations on the Past and Present States of that Country and its Inhabitants*. His journey from St Petersburg to Turku was made in 1816. Pinkerton's account of Finland is much more positive and favourable than that given by Wraxall, Carr, or Porter; unlike them, he was not a transit traveller, but genuinely wished to meet people. Crossing the Russian frontier he noted that 'as soon as one enters Finland, a higher degree of civilisation is very perceptible'. Another reason for the contrast is that Pinkerton was not a gentleman travelling and sleeping in his own carriage, but was accustomed to making do and roughing it. Because he was not troubled by the discomforts of travel he had leisure to take in and appreciate his surroundings.

British travellers often take their personal interests and enthusiasms with them to impose on their host country. Pinkerton is a striking example of the kind: everywhere he stopped, after enumerating the places of worship, his chief concern was the illegitimacy rates. At Hamina he was well pleased; of 253 births in 1819 only four were out of wedlock. In Porvoo, by contrast he was grieved to find an illegitimacy rate of 25%.

This preoccupation, fortunately, did not blind him to the beauties of the scenery:

Twenty miles from Friedriksham we crossed the stream Kymeny, near its beautiful cataracts; which, in two falls, have a descent of about thirty feet, from the granite bed of rock above to the surface of the boiling and foaming abyss below. The scenery all around is captivating. As we continued our route westward, the country seemed to increase in boldness, yet without ever rising into mountains. The masses of bleached granite scattered on the surface of the ground sometimes appeared, at a distance, like the mighty camp of a large army, or the immeasurable remains of some great metropolis. I was delighted to see the peasantry flocking, in small companies, from their scattered hamlets among the rocks, to their respective central parochial churches – the females carrying in their hand their Hymn-book and folded white pocket-handkerchief: all were in the national costume, the men in white russet coats, and the females in their striped stuffs and red stockings, all of their own domestic manufacture.

It is difficult to equate this colourful, picture-book image of the Finnish peasantry with the squalor described by most other travellers on this route. Despite his pleasure at the national costumes, Pinkerton's own chauvinism emerged during his visit to the village church at Pyhtää:

The paintings of the Apostles, on the front of the gallery, were rude beyond conception; the altar-piece, representing the institution of the Lord's Supper, was in the same style; and the wooden figures of our Lord and his Apostles were in the Finnish costume! There was a large wooden crucifix, and several other carved logs, added to the unsightly ornaments of the place.

He continued through Loviisa to reach Porvoo late at night. Here he met the Secretary and Directors of the 'Borga Bible Society'. One of the members told Pinkerton that

> it was still surmised, by many among among them, that the British and Foreign Bible Society had some weighty secret object hidden under the ostensible one, of giving Bibles to the poor. I endeavoured to set this worthy member right as to the simplicity of our object, and the purity of our motives.

As a missionary in Finland he wanted to 'have a better idea of its productions, and of the state of its inhabitants', so he boldly (considering that he knew no Finnish) branched off from the coastal route at Porvoo, travelling through Sibbo to Hämeenlinna. On balance he found much which impressed him:

> From Sibho we took the road for Vectles. I was surprised, after driving forty or fifty miles into the interior of the country, to find so many indications of culture – the corn fields well laid out – the pasturage marked off – the winter crop in bloom – the summer crop covering the clod; and, in the interval between sowing and haymaking, the peasantry, almost in every district, busily engaged in repairing the high roads. These, in general, are almost as good as our English roads, quite level, and covered with gravel and sand; only they are very narrow, insomuch that, in many parts, two ordinary carriages cannot pass. But I forget myself – these roads are made for their own convenience, and not for that of strangers. The only carriage used in Finland is a small two-wheeled car, drawn by one horse; which is made in the form of a gig, and narrow, so that two of them

can easily pass each other on their narrow roads.

After repeatedly visiting the huts of the Finnish peasants, I find that, in general, they are great strangers to the comforts of cleanliness: in this respect, their huts are even inferior to the *izba* of the poorest Russian. It is difficult to reconcile the general appearance of order and propriety in their fields and roads, and even in the external appearance of their houses, with this internal filth and disorder of every kind. Perhaps their rulers contribute greatly towards the former, but have no controul over the latter. Their poverty may help to account for it; – they are poor, and oppressed. And yet in the houses of peasants who seemed to be in more easy circumstances, there was not a bench clean enough to sit down on: and when I looked into their couches early in the morning, and saw the poor children lying no cleaner than their domestic animals, it was impossible not to desire an improvement in their household economy, proportioned to their attainments in husbandry.

I have never, during all my travels, been at such a loss for want of language, as in the two or three days that I travelled in the heart of Finland. I did not understand a syllable of what the people spoke, nor did they comprehend a word of what I said. It was rare to find a person who spoke Swedish (with such a one I could converse); and still rarer, one who knew a few words of Russ. Every thing, therefore, was transacted through the medium of signs; in which my young Russian servant was very clever, and sometimes amused me not a little by his ingenuity in making the people understand what he wanted.

Some parts of the country are very beautiful, particularly around the lakes, where the heights are covered with the golden-leaved silver pine; than which, at this season of the year, I know not a tree of richer colours. The cypress and olive of the Athenian groves are not to be compared with them for beauty.

After 'many hair-breadth escapes' on the narrow roads at night, Pinkerton joined 'the great road' at Somero:

When we arrived within twenty miles of Abo, we began to meet the country-people returning from the annual fair of that city, which is held for three days. This gave me an opportunity of making my observations on the sobriety of the Finns, as the whole strength of this virtue is put to the test on the peasants leaving a fair. More than 400 gigs or carts passed us during the last two stages. I observed that fewer instances of intoxication were seen in those whom we first met; so that the degree of drunkenness or sobriety might be measured by the later or earlier departure of the countryman from the fair. Among upwards of 1000 who passed us, the great majority were sober, and very decent in their appearance and behaviour. Three or four instances of sottish drunkenness, several of raving intoxication, and a few of staring and staggering wildness, were, however, to be observed as we drew nearer to the city. We arrived in Abo a little past midnight, and with some difficulty procured a place in the inn.

With drunkenness, as with illegitimacy, Pinkerton's interest seems to have been statistical rather than moral. The annual fair, which Clarke had witnessed in January, seemed to have moved to the summer.

Pinkerton saw the usual sights in Turku, and is, I think, the first of the travellers to have visited – or to have mentioned, even – the Observatory, 'a fine new circular building, on the top of a high granite rock; whence the view is extensive, over the Gulf of Bothnia, and the bare rocks of the neighbourhood'. He observes that '[t]he Russians have also built themselves a church in Abo, as indeed in most of the towns in Finland'. He describes the forwardness of the printing of the Finnish Quarto Bible, just completing an edition of 7500 copies. Pinkerton adds a footnote, part of a letter from Archbishop Tengström in 1827, informing him of the fire which had destroyed most of the town, including the copies and printing plates of the Bible; Pinkerton was commissioned by the Society 'to get an edition of 5000 Finnish Testaments printed for them'.

He notes that the university 'is conducted, in all respects, according to the rules of the Swedish Universities', and that lectures are 'given in the Swedish language'. There were about twenty professors, 'nearly all of them Finns, with salaries of about £120 per annum, and between two and three hundred students'. He does not mention meeting any of the professors, and he missed Bishop Tengström, who 'was gone to his country seat' for the summer.

Pinkerton's account ends here, presumably because he felt that he left Russia when he departed from Turku.

John Paterson

There was another British missionary in Finland at this time who was not, like Pinkerton, at 'a loss for want of language'. This was John Paterson, who, as far as I know, was the only traveller in this period to have learnt any Finnish: 'I knew something of the Finnish language, and the Swedish perfectly,' he claimed. Paterson was a Scot of humble background, an apprentice who educated himself so that he was able to study at Glasgow and Dundee Universities, and to become a Congregational minister. He became involved in northern Europe completely by accident: he had intended to do missionary work in India, but because the East India Company did not permit the transport of missionaries he took the 'unofficial route', and sailed to Denmark to get a boat on from there. During a long delay in Denmark he and his companion Ebenezer Henderson began, according to his biographer, 'to put forward such exertions as they could for the spiritual benefit of the inhabitants'. Eventually his superiors in Edinburgh wrote that it was 'their duty to give up thoughts of going to India, and endeavour to cultivate the field which Providence had opened for them in the north of Europe'. Paterson was in Copenhagen during the bombardment of 1807, and left a vivid account of it. He subsequently settled in Stockholm, distributing Bibles, supported but not employed by the British and Foreign Bible Society. His reminiscences were published after his death, edited with a Prefatory Memoir by William Lindsay Alexander, and entitled *The Book for Every Land* (1858).

Paterson was in Stockholm when Russia attacked Finland

in 1808; Russian troops crossed the frozen Gulf as far as Åland, and for a time threatened Stockholm. 'I could not but think that my lot had been cast on troublesome times,' he mused, fearing a repeat of his Copenhagen experience. He travelled as far as Tornio, on the land route to Turku, 'but the advance of the Russian army compelled [him] to retreat'. It was not until August 1811 that he crossed to Turku 'aboard a Finnish lump, a small vessel of peculiar construction, for carrying passengers rather than goods'. Bishop Tengström, whom he intended to visit, was away for two weeks, so Paterson spent this time making acquaintances in Turku; he returned there many times over the years. He was deeply impressed with the Bishop's combination of learning and humility; out of their meetings the Finnish Bible Society grew. When Paterson returned to Stockholm he records that 'the English vessels were exceedingly troublesome in the Gulf', waylaying and ransacking local boats for provisions in a form of soft-hearted piracy.

His next trip to Finland was in 1812; he set off in May and had a horrific eight-day journey across the broken ice – 'one of the most fatiguing journeys I ever made'. He had to travel on from Turku to visit the Bishop, rather unseasonably, at his summer residence. They fished together, and discussed the printing of the Finnish Bible. Later that year the Bible Committee in England offered him two hundred guineas and his expenses to visit Finland and to report on the possibilities of distributing Bibles there. Having got permission to set up a printing house for Bibles in St Petersburg, he moved there, and it was his base until he returned to Scotland in 1826. During these years he was 'connected with the work of translating and printing portions of the scriptures into Finnish, Georgian, Icelandic, Lappish, Lettish, Moldavian, Russ, Samogitian, and Swedish'.

Paterson returned to Stockholm to wind up his affairs and in July, with his Swedish wife, Katrine, set off for St Petersburg. He crossed Finland by way of Tampere and Porvoo. At Tampere he 'was struck with the facilities afforded in this locality for driving machinery by water power'. This visit was to have important consequences a few years later, when he returned here with a Scottish acquaintance.

During the fourteen years that he was based in St Petersburg, where the Russian Bible Society was founded in 1813, he made further journeys in Finland on his way to England in 1814 and in 1817. On the first occasion his route was via Vyborg, Lappeenranta, Hämeenlinna and Turku, but not trusting the ice he headed north to Pori and along the coast to cross the Gulf from Vaasa. The cold was intense:

> We had taken a large piece of excellent beef with us, to cut down as we needed it for steaks; but, alas! it got frozen, and would not cut with a knife, try as we might, nor even with the hatchet . . . Our wine was as obstinate as our beef and bread, for it, too, froze, and not a sip could we get till we melted it before the fire. It was not quite so clear or so tempting to look at it in its hardened state, standing upright in the glass.

They dined at Vaasa, and spent the night on the outermost island, so as to get an early start. 'I never spent a night in a more clean and comfortable inn,' he wrote. The description of crossing the ice is one of the best of many from this era:

> Next morning we were all astir by four, and after a hearty breakfast, we set out fully equipped for our long and rather dangerous journey across the ice. We had a clear stretch of between forty and fifty miles before reaching the nearest island. Besides our three sledges, our guides had their own, laden with provender for

their horses, provision for themselves, and all that was needed to overcome difficulties along the way, in case we met any, especially long deals to lay across any rents we might meet with in the ice. Those rents are not uncommon, and they are sometimes dangerous, for occasionally they are so wide, that even with the aid of the planks they cannot be crossed. In this case the traveller has to make a roundabout, until he finds a practicable crossing. The day was uncommonly fine, – quiet, calm, with bright sunshine. Men and horses made free use of the snow to slake their thirst as they passed on. The horses caught a mouthful of the snow without stopping. The path was well marked off with young trees. We were amused at the ice hills heaped one on another, sometimes to a considerable height. These were formed while the ice was yet in broken pieces, by the wind and the waves throwing one piece upon another. Our path wound among them, so as to find a level. We met with no obstruction to our progress.

About midday we stopped on the middle of the ice to rest the horses and feed them, and refresh ourselves. Having the night before prepared coffee, which I carried in a bottle in a warm place, I lighted my spirit-lamp apparatus in my sledge, and succeeded, notwithstanding the cold, in bringing it nearly to the boil. This appeared something like witchcraft to our peasants, who had never witnessed such an experiment in such a place. To us it was most refreshing. This over, we put fresh horses to our sledges, and again pursued our way, with the same success as in the former part of the day; and a little after dark arrived at an island on the Swedish side, not far from the main land, truly thankful to our heavenly Father, who had conducted us in safety thus far.

In 1817, again travelling in winter, he went via Kuopio to Oulu – the first Briton to record this route – and on to Sweden by land through Tornio. He travelled with with his 'Christian friend, Mr. George Brown', Dr Henderson and Mr Rutt; each traveller had his own sledge, and there was one just for provisions and luggage. He profited from his experiences from 1814 and made very thorough preparations: this time the beef was cut into steaks before it got frozen. The travellers were well-prepared in other ways:

> We took a good supply of cooked ox tongues, as they are the only flesh which, owing to their oil, do not get hard when frozen; also a good supply of rusks, which, from their being perfectly dry, do not freeze like loaf-bread . . . We had also a jar of minced veal, which we found excellent when warmed; then, some good portable soup; and, in addition, plenty of good wine and spirits. It must be remembered that we had a journey of 2,000 miles and more before us, a great part of it through the wildest part of Finland, where nothing could be got, especially in the winter season, and this winter was a very severe one. We were abundantly provided with warm clothing, so we feared not suffering from the intense cold.

The preparation went beyond the the provision of food, drink and clothing. The sledges were 'fitted up with lamps within, and stored with books, so that we could amuse ourselves with reading, whether by day or by night'. From Vyborg to Kuopio, he wrote, 'the road runs by a chain of beautiful lakes. They were now hard frozen, and formed an excellent road, quite level, and as smooth as glass'.

As on all his journeys, Paterson sought out 'pious' people wherever he went. He and his companions had a supply of

'Finnish Testaments' and 'embraced every opportunity of giving them to the people, who can all read'. 'They were received with tears of joy,' he adds. Paterson was actually able to describe the interiors of Finnish peasant houses; most travellers gave, at best, just a disgusted reaction:

The real Finnish houses are far from comfortable, especially in the winter time. They generally consist of only one very large apartment, with benches all round the walls, on which they sit during the day, and sleep, young and old, male and female, during the night. They have no windows, only a few oblong square holes cut in the walls, through which a little light finds access during the day, and as they have no chimney vents, through them also the smoke escapes. They are kept warm by a huge stove of stone or brick placed about the middle, and well supplied with firewood, of which there is a great abundance everywhere. As the square holes in the walls are cut about four feet from the floor, the smoke descends no lower, but all above is one thick cloud. Where we were seated we had a clear and tolerably pure atmosphere, but when we rose up, our heads were in the cloud. The smoke keeps perfectly on a level, and, when undisturbed, is motionless; but a wave with a hand sets it all in motion. It afforded a fine example of the clouds in the heavens, and seemed as if subject to the same laws . . .

As soon as it was light, if we found the people up, we stopped for breakfast. We soon had a blazing fire kindled, which might have roasted an ox; got boiling water, and made our own coffee with a spirit lamp; took out as much of our beefsteak as we thought we should need, quite hard frozen, but as it was immediately dressed in a pan over a blazing fire it had not time to putrefy, which it would have done if it had thawed gradually in a warm place. After breakfast we shaved and washed, and made ourselves comfortable for the day. We then pursued our journey until it got dark, when we stopped for dinner and supper and tea all in one. If we did not make tea, we had some of our portable soup prepared, and our minced veal warmed up, and perhaps a steak, with a glass or two of wine, which we required to have melted before we could get it out of the bottle, as it generally was in a state of ice, though not quite so solid as water would have been, for the spirit in the wine could not be frozen, but was contained in cells in the frozen mass. The wine was always found good, notwithstanding its being frozen. If we required anything in the middle of the day, or middle of the night, we had it always at hand in our sledges. About five in the morning we generally felt a little chilly, but taking about half a wine glass full of brandy the circulation was quickened, and the bodily warmth kept up till breakfast time. Thus by travelling night and day we got on quickly, and in forty-eight hours after leaving Wiborg we reached Kupio late on Saturday night, the 1st of February.

They did not, of course, travel on 'the sabbath', but spent it in Kuopio, calling on 'some pious individuals', and having 'much conversation with the Governor and other leading men about the Bible society'. The journey to Oulu was uneventful, but a couple of incidents Paterson thought worth recording:

One day we had nearly got into an awkward mess. I had an old vicious brute of a horse before my sledge. The boy who was driving was equally vicious in his way, and kept whipping the animal and making him gallop. I frequently spoke to him, and forbade him to whip the animal, but to no purpose. At last the animal, irritated by his conduct, gave him a kick with the whole force of his hind leg right in the middle of his forehead. He fell back into my lap, and I thought he was killed. After a few minutes he set up a fearful yell, which was joy to my heart, for, however discordant his cry, I was glad to find that he had still so much life in him. We got him up, examined the wound, a clean cut to the bone about three inches long. The nerves were laid bare, but they were apparently whole, and the bone did not seem injured. The wound was bleeding, but not profusely, as no vessel of any consequence was severed. We were two miles from any house. We bathed the wound and forehead with brandy, and tied it up with a handkerchief, and in a few minutes he was quite hearty . . .

Another day, my friend feeling stiff from being so long confined to the sledge, got out to run by its side for a little but coming on some bare ice he fell, and hurt the lower part of his back, which gave him considerable pain during the rest of the day and night. Next morning, after breakfast, I proposed that he should allow me to rub it well with strong brandy before the fire, in doing which the brandy on my hand took fire, and, without thinking, I clapped it to his back and set it on fire. He ran through the room calling for help, but the whole scene was so comic, that I was overwhelmed with laughter, and help could render none. However, it proved an effectual cure for the fall, leaving only a very small blister or two. These were the only adventures we had during our long journey.

Paterson records stops at Oulu and Kemi; at Tornio 'I did not find the clergyman . . . very zealous, but endeavoured to make him more so.'

He returned from England during the summer, for once making the journey in fine weather.

Paterson was a tireless worker for his cause, but does record one trip in Finland which was unashamedly 'a few days of recreation', sight-seeing with friends around Vyborg. As well as a glass works, and the famous quarry at Pyter-lahti, their 'grand expedition was to the famous waterfall':

> We arrived at the wretched village, near which the falls are situated, about the middle of the day. The post-house was the most miserable-looking place, in which it was impossible for four ladies and two gentlemen to lodge for a night; and yet, stay a night we must, if we were to attain our object.

The only 'tolerable house' (one room and a kitchen) belonged to the bailiff, who was away; Paterson's party bluffed and bullied their way into it for the night. The next day

> we went to see the falls, which were certainly magnificent. The water consisted of an immense cataract, which, for about half a mile, was pent up between rocks, in a very narrow bed and which did not fall perpendicularly, but rushed along an inclined plane of about forty-five degrees, with a fearful impetuosity . . . I never saw anything more grand. The whole scene was one of wild sublimity.

They returned to find that the bailiff and his wife had returned to their house, astonished to find that it had been commandeered. Paterson softened him up, and finally won his affection with a gift of Swedish, Finnish and Cossack Testaments. The next day they 'spent the forenoon in again visiting and admiring the falls and the surrounding scenery' before returning to Vyborg. Among Paterson's travels in

Finland these two days are of particular interest: well before the end of the century the Imatra rapids (not even named by Paterson) had become perhaps the prime tourist location in all Finland, the unspeakable distant post-house replaced by a luxury hotel overlooking the falls. Paterson's is the earliest description of Imatra which I have found.

In 1819 he set out on his most extended peregrination of Finland in order to complete the organisation of the Bible Society. His route was (in his original spellings) Reaholm, Wellmannstrand, Keropis, Krunenburg, Nyeslatt, Knopio, Sceonjaki ('a delightfully retired spot'), Wasa, Björneborg ('the clergy were not so zealous as they should be'), Tammerfers, Abo, Helsingfors, Borgo, Lovisa, Fredrickshavn, Wiborg. At Vaasa he was grieved to discover that in the provinces 'where the people are more enlightened they are less moral'. This he put down to their 'being better off in their worldly circumstances, and to their intercourse with Stockholm'. The Governor supported the formation of a 'Religious Tract Society for Wasa', and Paterson assumed that this would take care of the problem. From Vaasa they travelled to Pori and on to Tampere.

The visit to Tampere is of particular interest because Paterson was accompanied throughout this journey by a young Scottish friend from St Petersburg, James Finlayson, whose name, as a result of this visit, would become much more famous in Finland than Paterson's:

> We left Björneborg on the morning of the 17th, and travelling alongside of the fine river, abounding with salmon, at the mouth of which, on an arm of the gulf, the town is situated, we arrived next day at Tamerfers, and took up our abode at Hattampra, with my old friends, Mr. and Mrs. Lafren. This is one of the most beautiful

spots in all Finland, situated amidst extensive lakes, and in a fruitful district. Here we spent three happy days. My friend Finlayson was delighted with the place. He at once perceived that I had not over-rated it in my description to him, and my friend Lafren afforded him every information he required. The Emperor had visited the spot some days before, and greatly admired its waterfall. On our return to Petersburg, Mr. Finlayson applied to Government for the grant of a small piece of land, on which to erect a manufactory for spinning cotton, and other purposes, and a sufficient command of water for the purpose. All and more than he asked was granted; and here works have been erected, which employ some hundreds of poor people, and being now entirely in the hands of pious men, who compose the partnership, are a great blessing to the country, and to hundreds of poor, industrious people. This result of our tour was, of itself, a sufficient recompense for all our toil in this long journey. We had great difficulty in getting away from these good people, and when we did start, they accompanied us on our way about twenty versts. Before leaving, they took us to the top of a rising ground, and showed us a magnificent picture; all the beauties of nature, as it were, united in one grand view. On the top of this hill, we bade our friends farewell, and pursued our journey to the Government town of Tavastahus, of the same name.

Finlayson was granted special privileges to enable him to set up the factory, including the settlement of skilled British spinners, weavers and engineers. He sold the enterprise in 1836, but both the name and the philanthropic spirit of the founder have survived to the present day.

Åbo University had granted the degree of Doctor of

Divinity to Paterson in 1817. As far as I know he was the first Briton to be awarded a Finnish degree. Tengström, now Archbishop, had been the moving spirit behind this award, and was therefore very concerned, when Paterson arrived there, to find that he did not have his academic hat:

> The Archbishop remarked that I was wearing a travelling cap; and, in fact, I had no hat of any kind with me on this long tour. He asked me what had become of my doctor's hat? I told him I had two years ago paid them for one, but it had never been sent me, or, at least, had never come to hand. 'You cannot,' he said, appear on the streets of Åbo without one, as it will seem as if you put no value on the degree we have conferred upon you.' 'Well,' I replied, 'I have not one, and I am not disposed to pay twice for my hat.' 'In that case,' he answered, 'you shall have one of mine to wear while you are here.' The Archbishop was a very little man, and how his hat was to get on my head, or rather how my large head was was to get squeezed into his hat, was a question which at first puzzled us. On his producing it, however, it was found, on being tried, to fit admirably, and out I sallied into the streets under the hat of the Archbishop; to the great amusement of my friend Henderson.

Like Pinkerton, and unlike most other travellers of this era, Paterson did not set out to get through Finland as quickly as possible; he visited parts of the country which were far removed from the Great Coastal Road, and saw more of ordinary Finnish life than most other writers in this volume.

Sir John Bowring

John Bowring grew up in Exeter; it has been suggested that 'the presence of foreign traders on the Exeter quayside gave him the opportunity of learning and practising languages'. Whether that was so or not, he acquired a formidable reputation as a polyglot, and was hailed by Thomas Hood as 'man of many tongues' – he claimed to know two hundred languages and to speak one hundred of them. He was well-known in the early nineteenth century as a radical politician, editor of the radical *Westminster Review,* and a close friend and later biographer of Jeremy Bentham. In later life he became a Member of Parliament, and ended his career as Governor of Hong Kong.

During the 1820s he published a number of volumes of translations of the popular vernacular poetry of Europe, beginning with *Specimens of the Russian Poets* (1821). This was followed by translations of popular poetry from Holland, Spain, Portugal, Servia, Bohemia, Hungary and Fresland. These volumes had a political motive: as a radical, Bowring believed that 'Songs of the People' were a resource against tyranny:

> The poetry of the people is one of the most delightful resources and comforts of nations that have been subjected by strangers. In it they often give expression to thoughts, which would otherwise find no vent.

Bowring passed through Finland on his way back from a commercial trip to Russia early in 1820. His brief account of his journey in *Autobiographical Recollections* (1877), a posthumous volume edited by his son, seems indeed to be a recollection rather than a journal-based account:

> I travelled through its silent and solemn forests, looking at the tracks of the wolves on the snow beneath, and listening to the crashes among the trees of the dense woods whose branches, bound together by icicles, were shaken by the stormy winds.

'I found among the Finns,' he wrote, 'a civilisation far superior to what I anticipated.' He stayed in Turku where he met, among others, Archbishop Tengström. During the 1820s he was preparing a book of Finnish popular poetry in translation, and corresponding with Finnish scholars he had met who could help him. His correspondents in Turku included John Julin. Although this book never appeared, Bowring published some of the material in a long article, 'Runes of Finland', in *The Westminster Review* in 1827, which was the first extended presentation of Finnish literature in English. His impression of Finland under the Russian regime is markedly different from James's, and embodies his own powerfully radical opinions. Not until the end of the century would such views be expressed again:

> In my intercourse with the leading men, I found that they had, like the Poles, an earnest longing for the return of their independence, but they were fully convinced that it was hopeless to dream of any such felicity. The immense power of Russia, acting upon the weakness and the divisions of the several countries she has absorbed into her huge empire, has imposed a yoke which, heavy though it be, must be borne. These regions are no doubt among the 'oppressed nationalities', and the best that can be anticipated is that such concessions may be made by the wisdom and fore-thought of the Russian

government as will remove any fair grounds for popular discontent. It is not for us, who have imposed our dominion upon many a once independent people, to be hasty in condemning the usurpations of other powerful states. The progress of time may bring to many a nation the blessings of self-government, and may instil into the hearts of their conquerors the conviction that they may safely and wisely leave many of their dependencies to take care of themselves. That time is undoubtedly rapidly advancing as regards several of the British colonies, in some of which the influence of the mother country is practically almost annihilated.

In the University of Åbo, the most accredited Swedish authors are used as text-books, and some of the sciences which have been cultivated with special success among the Swedes, such as botany and chemistry, under the great names of Linné [Linnæus] and Berzelius, appeared to me to be the objects of particular attention among the Finlanders. A short time before my visit, a dreadful fire had destroyed the university library, and I had the pleasure, with the aid of friends, to send a pretty large collection of English literature, helping in a small way to fill the melancholy vacuum left by the ravages of the flames.

Bowring got his dates wrong in these memoirs, since the great fire of Turku was seven years *after* his visit. The other details are correct. He went to a lot of trouble to send English books, and several hundred of these are still in Helsinki University Library.

Bowring regarded his journey from Turku to Stockholm as one of his greatest adventures, and his account, though brief, is vivid:

In order to avoid the long and weary land journey round the Gulf of Bothnia, by Torneå, I engaged, at Åbo, a small boat with four men, and sledges to go on as far as possible, hoping in this way to cross to Sweden. We went on very well for six or seven miles, when the great chasms between the masses of ice (one of the horses having fallen through, and several of the men) induced us to send back the sledges, and to try to drag our little boat to the furthest possible point. The labour of hauling it thus for several miles, surrounded as we were on every side by hills of ice, and by large holes where the ice had been broken by the storm, was extreme, but we reached at last open sea, and launched our boat, hoping that our difficulties were over. We encountered, however, large islands of ice, and found the water freezing around us, so that we had soon to cut our way through ice an inch thick. The cold and frost increased, and at sunset we found ourselves completely frozen in, no land to be seen, cold and darkness over and around us, in an open boat, and in a latitude of 60 degrees. I had always found fortitude under bodily suffering, and my spirits did not flag. I wrapped myself in my wolf-skin and slept, thinking of my friends, the North Pole Expedition, and the second part of Don Juan. We had a couple of days' provisions, no compass, and our food was frozen to ice. I had once or twice expected, in the course of our land journey, that we should have been lost in the snow, but now I thought of a worse fate. I was calm, however, and rejoiced to think that nobody knew where I was who cared a pin about me.

We lay thus for nine hours, and at break of day were so fortunate as to discover an open sea before us, and, with the assistance of the wind, we cut through the ice, which had been much agitated through the night and was breaking around us, and reached again a space where we could use our oars. The Finn sailors seemed less pleased than I, for the ice islands, broken by the storm, were approaching us; and they feared that we might be carried away by them. However, amidst their crashing and noise, we made great progress, and drew near the coast of Sweden.

There are many passing references to Finland in Bowring's writings. One of the most intriguing is a letter from 1834 to George Borrow, who was planning to visit Finland: 'I am charmed with the thought of your taking to your bosom all those abandoned and desolate damsels.' Although it is very likely that Borrow did spend time in Finland, no one has come up with definite evidence.

Francis Bayley

Francis Bayley was educated at Eton and Cambridge, and spent his life in the law, sitting as judge of the Westminster County Court until his death at the age of ninety. His travel diary describes a journey he took as a young man in 1823–4. He went by sea to Kronstadt, took a steamer to St Petersburg, and then by 'diligence' (stage-coach) to Moscow, a four-day journey in each direction. He returned back through Finland to Stockholm then through Uppsala to Gothenburg, through Denmark and back to England via Hamburg.

He left St Petersburg on Thursday, 9 October, 1823, dined at Vyborg the next day, and, like several of the travellers on this route, viewed the granite quarry at Pyterlahti. On the following Saturday he records being 'tremendously bitten at the inn where I slept – Hogfars'. He left Helsinki on the 15th, was delayed by the rain at Kirkkonummi, and arrived in Turku on the 17th. He records 'Comfortable inn called the Societat'. He was advised to take a packet, sailing the next day, rather than the 'post road over the Åland islands', which most British travellers at this time took; it is therefore a different type of journey which he describes here. Most of the travellers of this period, as far as they describe food and drink at all, emphasise the hardness of the bread and the effect on the natives of the brandy. Bayley gives a mouth-watering description of the food and drink which can enhance a voyage, and relieve the tedium of being becalmed. He knew that he needed to carry his own provisions; during the voyage he learned how experienced travellers managed this.

Saturday 18

Put my things on board & provided myself with coffee sugar bread cold boiled beef & brandy for the voyage. Changed my money 670 rubles for which Mr. Levison gave me only 34 instead of 36 skillings each. I can safely pronounce him to be a great rogue. Sailed at 7 p.m. or rather we were towed down the river – a dead calm. Before we left Åbo I asked for a candle & my servant told me I had none. That I knew very well but I found that nothing was provided for me except the cabin & cold water. The captain as a favor gave me a candle.

Sunday 19

In the morning we found ourselves not a mile distant from Åbo – out of sight of the town but very near the castle. The scenery pretty – a light breeze sprung up but quite contrary, however we managed to get on slowly & by the evening had made 2 or 3 miles[;] we cast anchor in a very narrow passage between two islands – the islands & rocks are so frequent & the passage so narrow that it is impossible to sail by night – we were never more than ½ mile English from land – I was very lucky in the situation of my cabin too – the only way to it was thro' that of a gentleman, who having an estate in Finland, lived part of the year there & the remainder in Stockholm – so he made the passage twice every year, & he perfectly understood the way to travel with comfort – he was very well read in French & English, tho he could not so well pronounce the latter, but being fond of English & naturally very hospitable, he made me dine & drink tea with him every day – his name Assessor Loffman & a more pleasant fellow could not be – he certainly was well prepared. He had

6 or 7 loaves of brown bread made of wheat & rye which were excellent & never spoiled by keeping, & some kegs of good fresh butter – some Swedish brandy flavoured like Maraskino & excellent – a boiled leg of pork – roast lamb – 12 lbs of beef for steaks – 4 or 5 tongues – 4 or 5 cold fowls boiled and others raw, a pot of jelly for soup another of cranberries, to eat as sauce to the fowls – a large tureen full of stewed apples, a box of almond fritters, a pot of small fish like anchovies to eat by way of relish before dinner, 2 dozen of wine but as he frequently lamented only two bottles of por-ter – the wine of different sorts, madeira, red & white Port & a delicious kind of sweet wine – to this stock he added mustard – pepper – salt – vinegar – tea – sugar – coffee, cups & saucers, plates, knives & forks, nap-kins. We generally added to this perch which we could almost every day get fresh, & his man was an excellent cook, dressing the perch & beefsteaks admirably – it is quite astonishing how much the tediousness of a voy-age is relieved by a pleasant companion & good food, as the captain did not provide anything for his passen-gers there was none of that unpleasant smell always met with in our packets, & the comfort of having a cabin to one's self is no trifle.

Wednesday 22

Attempted to sail but were driven back but we ran up alongside the land so as to walk ashore on a plank from the ship – dined on shore & after dinner scribbled the following – in the house of the principal inhabitant of an island or rather rock in the Gulf of Bothnia about 8 miles from Åbo in company with a Swedish gentle-man whose cabin is next to mine and with whom I have by that means become acquainted. We have made

an excellent dinner on perch (arboren) & part of the
Swede's travelling stock, Maraskino, chicken, tongue &
cranberries (lingan) -- almond fritters – apples the produce of the island (quite impossible – it must have been
an island near) & coffee which is always to be found
& is as universally used in this part of the world as tea
in England. The House extremely good – smart white
clean tablecloth – white delft plates – silver spoons –
the room as usual contained a bed but in shape like an
English one except that at the bottom of it from ceiling
to the floor is a cupboard – walls papered & a cupboard in one corner – guns placed on shelves nailed to
the beams of the ceiling – among them 2 firelocks – immensely heavy wooden chairs of the same shape as my
tutor's arm chair in the pupil room at Eton, but without
arms, & every thing the same as in England except the
stove & that too is open – the table of oak like that
in my father's kitchen but better polished – in another
corner a clock – 3 geraniums & a very large plant in
one window – out of this room a smaller room a bed
room – across the passage is the family room, there are
3 other buildings forming a little square, that on the
left contains a single room much like this & quite as
good – looking out on the water. This is on an island
which much more that any I ever saw may be said to be
merely a rock.

The next day there was a favourable wind; they set off
early, 'were searched by the Russians at their last station',
and 'at nine p.m. anchored at the first Swedish station' having sailed 150 miles in the day.

This extract is of special interest because it comes from a
genuine diary, written with no view to publication. Bayley
may be taken as representative of many men who travelled

to these parts but left no record. One may guess that most of the accounts in this volume are based on diaries and note-books such as this, but written up and embellished for pub-lication. Bayley writes without any sense of an audience, and perhaps as a result his account is free of the chauvinism and the need to show off a superior taste, which is common among many fashionable travellers of the time.

Captain George Matthew Jones

'Entering the naval service at a very early age', as he put it, George Matthew Jones pursued a full-time naval career, sailing with Nelson and giving distinguished service in the Adriatic. In 1818, at the age of about thirty-three, he was promoted to the rank of Post Captain, and this gave him the means to follow his own interests. Travelling with his two brothers, he set out to visit the principal European seaports with which he had had contact during his career at sea. These travels took place in the years 1820–24, and landed him in Finland in September 1822.

He kept a regular journal of his travels, and published it in two volumes in 1827 as *Travels in Norway, Sweden, Finland, Russia and Turkey.* In his introductory remarks he modestly presents himself as a latecomer in a harvest field where there was little left to glean. 'Yet,' he writes, 'no field is so well cleared, that by diligence and attention a sheaf may not be collected.' He was aware that in Scandinavia he was travelling in the shadow of Clarke, 'than whom a more beautiful and correct writer is not to be found', but felt that after a quarter of a century enough had changed to justify a further account.

As might be expected, Captain Jones casts a nautical eye about him, and describes ships and navigation in some detail. He had always been actively engaged in naval affairs, and as a result he had, in contrast to many of the British travellers of the time, a very clear understanding of the political situation in the 1820s, as Finland adjusted to Russian sovereignty. He writes knowledgeably and objectively about the effects of this political change on religion, on military arrangements, and on trade.

The journey from Stockholm was a mixture of conviviality and fear. There were eleven passengers, six of them women, and 'arrangements, satisfactory to all parties, were soon made relative to the mode of living, sleeping, &c.' Jones shared a cabin with his brother, and they travelled

> in a steam-boat, commanded by an Englishman, and having an engine, said to be of a fifty horse power, but which unfortunately on the day of need did not prove half of the force.

Jones is rather negligent in not describing the boat, which must have been the first steamer on this route. It was a wood-burner, and clearly a species of hybrid, since after the failure of the engine, it escaped a rocky fate by use of its sails. Eight years later John Barrow made the journey from Turku to Stockholm by sail, reporting that the steam boat had gone aground the previous year. It very nearly did so on this occasion: the boat blew off course, and the pilot, as a result, could not recognise where they were. They rode out the storm until dawn, when the anchor-chain broke; they escaped from being shipwrecked on the rocks by a lucky change of wind, and were able to resume the 'straight or turnpike-road, which our pilot so well knew'.

Jones gives a fascinating description of the boats ('swamps') that traded between the islands and Stockholm; they seemed to his professional eye virtually unseaworthy, with their loads of timber 'piled up ten or twelve feet' and 'a well for carrying over live fish'. He had a very low estimate of the 'maritime skill and enterprise' of the Swedes, and felt that it was only good fortune which got him alive through the archipelago to Turku:

As they never think of starting without a fair wind, and the vessels are by no means calculated to encounter bad weather, they cannot be termed either a hardy or expert race of seamen: in all probability the generality of them are of the same description as our pilot proved to be of, that is to say, bold and confident in fine weather and a fair wind, but once out of the straight road or encountering difficulty, helpless and desponding – for during our danger he appeared more like an alarmed passenger than the man to whose skill and judgement our safety was intrusted.

Not all travellers during the rest of the century got off as lightly as Jones did when crossing Russia's new western border in the Gulf of Bothnia:

In the evening we came to the first Russian custom-house, where a mere form of examination took place, but our passports were sent to the guard-vessel, a Russian sloop of ten guns. Having replenished our fuel (wood), we proceeded a few miles further, and then anchored for the night, which we passed under much pleasanter circumstances than the last. At the custom-house we procured some excellent perch, off which we supped. In the morning at six we started, with the wind from the northward, but with rainy, dirty weather. After passing innumerable islands, some of them well wooded, others distinguished by windmills, and only one by a church, we arrived at five o'clock at Abo, under unfavourable circumstances as to weather; still the appearance of the town and port was extremely interesting. With little interruption from either the custom-house or police, we soon had our carriage and ourselves well lodged at a large and good inn, called the Society

House. As soon as we arrived, Mr. Augustine, a relative of some of the female passengers, came on board, when they were pleased to say, they felt obliged to us for our attention paid to them during the voyage. Mr. Augustine therefore insisted upon our drinking tea with him, and made us promise to take a family dinner with him on the next day, the particulars of which I shall relate in due time.

Jones's account of Turku certainly has something to add to what earlier travellers had recorded, especially with its account of a Finnish family party. He spent a lot of time at the cathedral, and, like Porter, admired the organ (but thought that it was 'rendered ridiculous by the figure of the donor, painted at full length in the centre of the case'.) He saw the university perhaps at the height of its fame, and was full of praise for the buildings: 'the hall is really a magnificent room . . . The cornices and ornaments are beautifully executed'. It was not only the buildings which impressed him:

> The professors are numerous, and are said to be well paid, and to enjoy a good reputation. The students have the privilege of wearing a sword when in full dress, which is considered a very honourable distinction to those who are not in the army.

His only misgivings concerned the observatory:

> The observatory being the most northern in the world, and on the same meridian as that at the Cape of Good Hope, excited great interest, and we hastened to visit it. The situation, on a rock above the town, is admirably commanding. The building is hardly finished, and we were quite shocked to find a magnificent set of

astronomical instruments, just received from Rieffeder and Co., of Munich, lying about half unpacked, and so exposed as to be at the merciless examination of every person whom the attendant, a common soldier, might introduce. We inquired for the astronomer, but were told that, as the observatory was not quite ready, he did not attend: I fear, when he does, the instruments will be so deranged as to be useless. The view is most extensive and varied, though the country appears very steril.

He found Turku very hospitable, and recorded the family dinner with the Augustines in appreciative detail:

On the day after our arrival, we repaired at two o'clock to the house of Mr. Augustine, in order to partake of his family dinner, but were surprised to find a party of twenty-four assembled; he however assured us that they were all relations: some of the females were very fine, handsome women. After partaking of *snaps*, an elegant dinner was served; there were removes innumerable: a good deal of wine was drunk, and we expected to retire, as is customary in Sweden, but, to our astonishment, the English mode of taking off the cloth and renewing the table with a dessert and wine was adopted, Mr. Augustine informing us that he had been in England and admired our customs. He then directed a bumper to be filled, and drank to the health of the King of England, with three times three. At the end of the roar, our astonishment and sense of his politeness were still further excited, by a full military band striking up 'God save the King.' We of course expressed our sense of the honour, and proposed toasts that we thought would be most agreeable to him; in this way the merry glass circulated till six o'clock, when dancing commenced, which was kept up with great spirit till near ten, when we again returned to the pleasures of the table, which with singing and toasts were continued till near midnight, when we were unwillingly allowed to retire from this family party, at which it is impossible that more hospitality or polite attention could have been shown; and we felt most sensibly the honour done to England, and to ourselves as Englishmen.

His observations and interests in the town were not confined to the well-to-do:

We were a good deal amused with the servant-maid at the Society House. Although pretty, she was dreadfully sulky, and we could neither extort an answer nor a smile from her, till just before our departure, when taking away something, she was greatly embarrassed how to open the door, from having her hands full: I immediately rose from table and opened it, when she felt the undeserved civility, and expressed her thanks in so different a way from her former manner, that she did not appear the same person – such is the contrast between amiableness and moroseness. But that you may not, from this anecdote, suppose that the Finnish damsels are all of her disposition, I must tell you, that the morning after our arrival I was surprised and awakened by a very amiable and pretty fruit-girl coming into my room, and offering to sell apples and plums: so difficult is it to form an opinion of character from one or two instances; for never was a greater contrast between two women of the same town.

After this agreeable sojourn in Turku they continued their journey. Some fellow travellers tried to persuade them into joining forces, for greater security, because of rumours of escaped convicts on the road. Jones had his own interpretation of this:

> We could not help feeling that he trusted much to our being Englishmen, of whom, in this part of the world, a very high opinion is entertained.

They declined the invitation, and soon after noon departed on the thirty-five-mile drive to Salo:

> From a hill about two miles from Abo, there is a curious bird's eye view of the town, which has a singular effect, from the diversity of the surrounding scenery: most of the houses, as in Denmark, have white chimneys. The extraordinary number of small windmills, both near the town and during the whole of the day's journey, attracted a good deal of attention; it appears to be the custom for every person to grind his own corn. We passed many neat looking country boxes.

Their first night on the road, at Salo, was tolerable:

> we arrived at a dirty post-house about seven o'clock; however, they gave us clean beds, and cooked a couple of grouse for our supper, so that we had no reason to complain of our treatment, particularly as the people were civil and obliging.

No other traveller has given such a full account of this part of the Great Coastal Road, or made it sound as attractive. They were driven by their servant, 'a very intelligent young man' they had hired in Sweden. Despite the unpredictable quality of the accommodation offered by the post-houses, Jones was delighted by the variety and picturesqueness of the landscape, which they saw in fine autumn weather:

Michaelmas day proved beautiful, and being Sunday, the road near Lembala was much enlivened by a number of equestrians and pedestrians repairing to church. They were all very well dressed; the women wearing their hair neatly done up, and enclosed behind in green silk or satin bags. The church inside was in a neglected state, but crowded to excess, the men and women occupying different sides. The inhabitants of the Duchy of Finland are Lutherans. Equipages do not appear to be common, for a gentleman seeing I was in a carriage, inquired if I was an ambassador.

Half way between Lembala and Svenskby, we came to a steep hill in a thick wood, which neither encouragement nor coercion would induce our horses to mount. After many ineffectual attempts, we were obliged to send the driver on, in order to bring fresh horses, which he did at the expiration of two hours, which we had passed not without some apprehension that the predictions of our former timid companion might have been verified; for certainly there never was a spot better calculated for such deeds. However, nothing happened, and we arrived safely at Mjolbolsta about eight o'clock, where we were miserably lodged. A number of peasants of both sexes were collected, and enjoying themselves in dancing and drinking: there was nothing graceful in the dancing; indeed I have never witnessed less at a country fair in England, which is saying a good deal. We made only forty-five miles during the day, the road being deep sand, which appeared the more extraordinary as on each side were rocks and trees, the latter consisting of pines, firs, and birch rather dwarfish; and, as the day before, we passed good looking houses, cattle, and crops of rye.

Monday proved delightful weather, and we made good one Swedish mile an hour, arriving at Helsingfors at five o'clock. The road till reaching Thaikes was something like that described in the north of Germany. Indeed, there does not appear to have been any attempt to form a road, except by cutting down trees, leaving sufficient space for carts and cattle to pass. It then became good till approaching the capital, when it was much cut up by traffic, although the country became rocky and steril. We did not pass many villages or churches; but now and then good-looking seats, or houses of country-gentlemen, appeared at a distance; indeed, they occurred more frequently than in either Denmark, Sweden or Norway: many of them were lofty, having even attics.

The post-houses in general are very bad, and the yards so deep with mud, &c., that a causeway of plank is obliged to be thrown across, in order to admit of approach to the house, which seldom affords a better entertainment than ham, eggs, and rye bread, the latter not eatable.

In a very few years Helsinki had grown in importance. Now the capital, and seat of government, it had

assumed a very imposing appearance, from the number of government buildings which are in progress, and are mostly constructed of brick stuccoed white. The senate-house is of great extent, with a staircase which does honour to the architect, Mr. Engel, a Prussian. He has been employed seven years, upon designs for improving and embellishing the town; he had the goodness to show us some of the plans, 'Approuvé par l'ordre supérieur de S. M. l'empereur, le prince Volskonsk'.

They lodged with Madamoiselle Chat, where they were 'extremely well treated, at a moderate price'. Jones spent a good deal of time exploring the fortress on Suomenlinna, and gives a catalogue of the ships to be found there. He was as observant of the military situation on land, as he had been of the seamanship on Gulf of Bothnia. He approved of the reduced 'military establishment', which had freed money for other projects in Finland. He comments on points of military etiquette, and describes in detail a formal ceremony, the flogging of a prisoner by a whole company of soldiers:

> Just before sun-set, a body of about two hundred and fifty soldiers marched out of the town; we followed them, and shortly afterwards saw a prisoner conducted from the barracks. The troops presented arms, a paper was read to the prisoner, after which they formed two deep, face inwards, with open ranks, and had thick twigs served out to them. The culprit was then stripped, his hands tied to the but-end of a musquet, the barrel of which was held tightly under the right arm of a sergeant, the drums began to beat, and in this manner the prisoner passed twice down and twice up the ranks; thereby receiving about one thousand lashes. The soldiers appeared to lay it on sharply, and with good will, many of them laughing and joking as he approached . . . His back, and particularly his arms, were a good deal cut, the blood flowing freely. The soldiers marched off singing, the prisoner was conducted to the hospital, while the twigs were carefully collected, and no doubt, put in pickle, for future service.

The English observers interpreted this as an instance of a regimental activity 'producing an *esprit de corps*'!

As they returned from witnessing this spectacle, they observed a very different sort of military occasion, one whose purpose Jones did not immediately understand:

> Walking past the barracks, we were attracted by a most extraordinary spectacle, which we have since found to be simply the operation of a Russian bath. A whole regiment came out, carrying green boughs in their hands; on arriving at a house from which steam and smoke were issuing, they stripped perfectly naked, and entered it. After remaining a short time, they came out, their bodies smoking, and as red as scarlet, and immediately ran into the sea, for a couple of minutes, then re-entered the house for a little while, after which they put on their clothes, and returned quite fresh to the barracks.

Jones's account of the rest of his journey adds only a little to what earlier travellers have described. After a brief delay at Porvoo, caused by the postmaster being buried ('All the windows of the house had snow white curtains, tied with black riband'), they stopped at Loviisa where 'there is no good post house, but we were well accommodated at a private dwelling belonging to Madame Bergman, who treated us with kindness'. During the next day's journey Jones picked up an interesting anecdote:

> About eighteen miles from Lovisa, near Pyttis, we passed the boundary between the old and new Finland, by a bridge over the river Alberfors. It is said, that the ex-king of Sweden, having caused the arms of that country to be painted on the Russian end of the bridge, it formed one of the pretexts for the war, which ultimately cost him the whole of the Duchy.

In Hamina they found that most of the houses had burned down a year earlier, and 'very little has been done to rebuild them, or even to clear the ruins, so it presents one of the most melancholy spectacles it is possible to imagine'. Unexpectedly, in such an unpromising place, they 'had excellent broth, roast beef, and bread, for dinner'. An attraction which other travellers had mentioned but not described, was a visit to the quarries at Pyterlahti. They felt that they risked their necks on the journey, but were 'amply repaid for it, by finding the operation of wedging out a block of granite of fifty-six feet in length, by six feet three inches diameter, in full activity'. These were intended for 'the Isaac's church' in St Petersburg. After dining at 'a very good post-house' at 'Kiskila' they reached Vyborg, where 'we appeared to have passed to a different race of people in every respect'.

Of the many British travellers who took the Great Coastal Road Jones was certainly one of the most observant and open-minded. His strength as a writer is that he is as much concerned with the journey as with the arrival. He travelled, too, at an interesting moment of Finnish history: the great fire of Turku was still five years in the future, but the great building activity which he records in Helsinki was in any case announcing that Turku's days of fame and importance were now over.

Jones's assessment of Finland's political situation after 1809 is especially astute; he believed that 'the Emperor Alexander' was extraordinarily 'disinterested and generous' towards Finland, but saw that all the benefits were 'held by an unstable tenure, the will of the sovereign'. Finland would find no useful friends should 'a future emperor' withdraw her privileges. He foresaw that 'Finland might become the point through which Russia would be vulnerable'.

Arthur de Capell Brooke

The attractions of Finnish Lapland for British travellers seem to have faded as the eighteenth century came to its end; more than a quarter of a century had passed before the next British traveller recorded crossing the Polar circle. Major Brooke, educated at Magdalen College, Oxford, and heir to a baronetcy, belonged to what was now becoming the older tradition of exploration, as opposed to travelling. He was a founder member of the Travellers Club, and of the Raleigh Club, which later merged with the Royal Geographical Society. He spent several years in Norway and Sweden, principally in the Arctic areas, and published two significant accounts: *Travels through Sweden, Norway and Finmark, to the North Cape in the Summer of 1820* (1823), and *A Winter in Lapland and Sweden* (1826). Although these books were – and are still – well-regarded, they have only a small place in this survey: only the last stages of his winter travels took Brooke into Finland. He was returning from the North Cape and crossed the Norwegian border near Muonio, fifty miles south of Kautokeino. From there he followed the Muonionjoki towards Tornio, on his way to Stockholm.

'Russian Lapland', as he termed it, offered immediate attractions at 'Hättan':

> We were hospitably received by the peasants, and a blazing fire, which was quickly made upon the hearth, preparations for cooking, and two fine Finland girls who also attended upon us, were indeed pleasant sights.

Brooke prided himself on his skill as a driver of reindeer,

and his is the only account of reindeer sledges in Finland which I have found:

> I found indeed that the deer had little need of being urged forward at first setting off; on the contrary, no restraint whatever had scarcely any effect in checking their eagerness to get on.

He was disappointed that after a few days horses could 'be procured for travellers' which he considered a 'tame' form of transport.

Brooke is a descriptive writer of unusual ability, and coming, here, among the predominantly factual and often prosaic accounts of southern Finland from the 1820s, his poetic impressions offer a welcome contrast:

> Evening approached with unusual splendour; the starry vault of heaven glittered with redoubled brilliancy, and the scene altogether was in an extraordinary degree imposing and magnificent. The frost was at this time intense: myriads of lights twinkled above with a brilliancy peculiar to these high northern latitudes, beautifully recalling to the mind the words of the poet: –
>
> > 'The full, ethereal round
> > Infinite worlds disclosing to the view,
> > Shines out intensely keen, and all one cope
> > Of starry glitter glows from Pole to Pole.'
> >
> > THOMSON's *Winter*
>
> It is difficult to describe the singularly vivid coruscations of many of the heavenly bodies, changing from flame colour, or orange, to that of a deep ruby, and each ray being distinctly conveyed to the eye through the pure surrounding ether. The flashings of the northern lights began also to play around us. A pale sheet of flame first streamed from the zenith. Its quivering fires

then darted swiftly along the heavens, and increased the sublimity of the scene; while the planet of night, riding high in the firmament, cast a mild and pensive lustre. As there had been a hoar frost, every spray glistened as if pendant with countless gems; and the gay sparkle of innumerable crystals from the surrounding illumination brought to the recollection the tales of fairy-land. It seemed almost as if we were passing through an enchanted forest and that Nature was displaying to us her magic wonders, to cheer the hours of the night. With our strange figures thickly encrusted with frost and rime, and hurrying silently along, we had less the appearance of men than of unearthly beings, or a band of goblins skimming the waste to perform their midnight orgies, and 'dance with the Lapland witches.'

'Fine writing' rarely goes further than this. Brooke showed appreciation also of less dramatic scenes, as in this description of sunless Lapland daylight:

The appearance of the sky about mid-day was strikingly beautiful, the whole face of it being overspread with a vermilion blush from the reflected light of the sun below the horizon; while the pale beams of the moon appearing in the midst of it, threw an air of indescribably softness around.

His response to seeing naked 'Finlanders' together in a sauna at Jarhois has been quoted in the Preface. This intrepid traveller showed himself to be a coward when he was given the opportunity actually to try the sauna himself:

There being a bastuen [bastu is Swedish for sauna], or vapour bath, my travelling companions, with the exception of Frue Klerck, took advantage of its refreshing powers after their journey, and were bathed by the young women of the house. This curious operation is invariably performed by females, and those the youngest of the family. One of the bathers, on the present occasion, was a good-looking girl of about seventeen. If I had not been so greatly occupied as I was, I should have been tempted, perhaps, to try the effects of the bath; and to have undergone the rubbing process, which is the most important feature of it, performed by so pretty a hand. The truth is, besides being busy, I did not quite like the idea of having this ceremony performed in the presence of so large a party, and which would seem to require no small degree of privacy. I therefore determined to pay a visit to the *bastuen* on some future occasion; and while the others were steaming, I proceeded to look at the church, at the distance of about half a mile.

At Parkajoki Brooke's driver got so drunk that he fell off the sledge, 'but the night being dark, I did not discover it until some time afterward, the horse following the other sledges as usual'. The route was that taken by several of the earlier travellers, through Tapojärvi, Kolari, Jarhois and Pello. By the time he reached the Gulf of Bothnia, the magic of Lapland had entirely vanished:

The appearance of the town of Torneå, which we gave a good look at the following day, is in no way prepossessing. Indeed, it struck me as being as forlorn and miserable a place as any I had yet seen.

Captain James Edward Alexander

Alexander was also a soldier, not, like Brooke, heir to a baronetcy, but a specialist in his profession, commanding a regiment in the Crimean War. He was also also a noted explorer, knighted in 1838 after an expedition in Africa. After studying at Sandhurst he (in his own words) 'joined the establishment at Chatham, for instruction in Military Field Works'. He then 'availed himself of a year's leave of absence from his late regiment [the 16th Lancers] to extend his knowledge of his profession, by visiting some of the Continental armies'.

His travels took him as far as the Black Sea, and what he saw of the Imperial fleet and the army in the field there made his account topical when it was published in 1830, a time when there was public interest in the Turkish theatre of war. His book has a crowded title-page: *Travels to the Seat of the War in the East, through Russia and the Crimea, in 1829. With Sketches of the Imperial Fleet and Army, Personal Adventures, and Characteristic Anecdotes.*

His route was via Hamburg and Travemünde, then through Estonia to St Petersburg. He continued by way of Moscow to the Crimea. Here he met Arthur Young (son of the Rev. Arthur Young, the agricultural writer), who was farming in Georgia, and who himself travelled through Finland early in 1814 and possibly on other occasions. After being arrested as a spy and detained for a month at Sebastopol, Alexander made a winter journey back to St Petersburg, where he was received at court. He passed through Finland on his way to similar receptions in Stockholm and in Copenhagen, finally returning home through Holland and France.

He was already accustomed to winter travelling, so the February journey from St Petersburg to Turku by sledge was undertaken with little fuss – indeed, he clearly found it exhilarating to travel at speed 'by night as well by day', lit by 'starlight, and occasionally the vivid coruscations of the aurora borealis':

The journey was not unattended with danger: for besides the wolves, which are often to be met with in troops on the roads, and not unfrequently in a rabid state, (even in the depth of winter,) from the frost acting on their teeth, the lakes were not always safe at night, when we deviated from the line indicated by the fir branches; and several times, in descending the hills with great velocity, if there was any defect in the steerage of the sledge, it would slide to one side, upset, and send us with our portmanteaus into the snow wreaths by the road-side, where the severe blows we got from the different articles of baggage would make our bones ache for many hours after.

But notwithstanding these mishaps we travelled gaily onwards. The drivers of the sledge were of all ages, and of both sexes: a decrepit old man would be succeeded by a buxom girl; and, as the Finns are very fond of music, they continually struck up the most simple and wild airs: and sometimes they were so touched by their own singing that the tears would stream down their cheeks. Occasionally I could get no driver at all; but, after a fresh horse had been put to, the peasant would hand me 'the ribbands,' point out the road, and I would set off with a shout, ploughing up the snow with the glowing skates of the sledge, and cracking the short whip as the signal for other sledges to keep the proper side. Although the cold was still intense, and the face of nature

was bound up in thick-ribbed ice, and pervaded by a
Sabbath stillness, yet, from the excitement of driving at
a rapid rate, the bracing air and the ever varying scenes
we passed, we set frost and ennui at defiance.

His account mentions just one stop before Turku: from
Helsinki he viewed the Suomenlinna fortress only from a
distance, so as not to 'incur suspicion by asking leave'.

Alexander has a particular importance in this chronicle as
the first British traveller to describe Turku after the devastat-
ing fire of 1827; his account of the city is a grim contrast to
earlier descriptions:

> *Abo*, at the union of the Gulfs of Bothnia and Fin-
> land, presented a most melancholy spectacle. It formerly
> occupied a ridge of rocks and a plain near a small river:
> but a short time ago a dreadful fire consumed nearly
> the entire city, consisting of a few brick, but principally
> of wooden houses. The cathedral escaped; but the uni-
> versity and other public buildings fell a prey to the de-
> vouring element. Never did I see such desolation and
> ruin. On every side the eye wandered over the black-
> ened remains of habitations, amongst which might be
> seen, at long intervals, workmen employed clearing out
> the foundations, and preparing for the construction of
> new streets.
>
> I had a letter to a Swedish merchant in Abo, and I
> found him at a country house at some distance from
> the town. Many of the respectable families had subur-
> ban retreats, in which they lived after the great confla-
> gration; and those who were burned out of house and
> home sought shelter in the neighbouring towns and vil-
> lages till Abo again rose from its ashes.
>
> M. Kinjelen took me in the evening to an assembly:

it was held in a house which had been saved from the flames; and here were congregated the beauty and fashion of this remote corner of Europe. The language was principally Swedish; and the fair-haired daughters of the North were attired after an antiquated fashion of dress; but their manners were frank and open. The hand of the men too was freely extended for a hearty shake: no solitary finger presented, as is the wont of the *beau monde, aujourd'hui,* but a good hard fist, and every bone of it. Neither was there any walking through the figure of the dance, a species of quadrille; but both sexes exerted themselves to the uttermost, showing great activity and animation to corresponding music.

Alexander was alive to the attractive appearance and manners of the ladies, but, as befitted a soldier, seemed to appreciate especially the no-nonsense directness of the men.

Although he claimed to have gone through 'fire, frost and plague' to collect the material for his book, Alexander comes over as the sort of traveller who never gets dismayed or alarmed. His appreciation of the beauties of the countryside is more extravagant than that of most of his contemporaries'. It is difficult to credit that the amenities of the route from Turku to Åland could really have been so completely transformed since Porter's dreadful experiences some twenty years earlier:

The scenery, after leaving Abo, was more beautiful than before. The pine-forests were boundless: many of them *intactæ securi*, and they occupied a broken and diversified country. In retired spots were the hamlets, and churches, with their high roofs and wooden belfries. The interior of the houses was hung with nets and the implements of husbandry, in fabricating and repairing which the men were employed. A raised and open fire-place occupied the place of the close Russian peach box-bedsteads, the shelf of the Muscovite peasantry; and the hum of the spinning-wheel accompanied the plaintive airs of the maidens. Occasionally a pastor would be found in the cottages, partaking of the rural fare of milk and *knacké brud,* instructing his parishioners in their moral duties.

Alexander's account of winter travelling over the ice to Stockholm is the only one in this collection which makes the journey actually sound fun. Even the dangers of a stormy passage through the broken ice is described like a jolly adventure. Alexander is seen here as yet another traveller who on occasion sees Finland through literary spectacles, in this case English Romantic pastoral rather than classical Greek:

The Aland Islands are many hundreds in number: some are mere rocks of granite; but the larger are well wooded, and cultivated by the industrious inhabitants. When benumbed with cold, after a long drive, it was really quite refreshing to arrive at night at one of the comfortable log-houses of the farmers, (through the windows of which was seen the light of a blazing hearth,) and on entering, to be welcomed by the hospitable inmates. The ruddy master of the house would be observed enjoying his 'home-brewed' and a pipe at a clean board: the mistress would be superintending the sewing, knitting, and spinning of the maidens, or giving directions for the supper; and the young men, each in his corner, or round the fire, would be plying their different trades of tailor, carpenter, or shoemaker: and, besides these, each householder is his own miller, baker, and brewer. The Alanders are allowed by the Russian

Government the free exercise of their ancient customs and privileges, and there did not appear to me a more happy and contented race than these islanders.

It is difficult to equate this idealised picture of rustic contentment with the descriptions of squalor and destitution given by some of the earlier travellers, and even more difficult to believe that his final stop, Signildsskär, was the same 'naked rock' where Porter had experienced such 'desolation and horrors':

> Signilshare is occupied by a few log-houses and defended by a couple of cannon. Our hostess, though very drunk, was most attentive to our comforts, and told long stories of accidents on the ice in winter; of seal hunters miserably perishing; of others drifting about for weeks on floating ice; of the crew of an English vessel, which had been wrecked on one of the islands when the frost set in last winter; and of the Captain and sailors being with her for three weeks, and nearly eating them up, and at last threatening to kill her cow. Some English oaths were occasionally introduced in her conversation, which served to beguile the winter's evening,
>> While, shook to notes
>> Of native music, the respondent dance
>> And rustic mirth went round.

These lines of verse are quoted – in fact, misquoted – from James Thomson's *Winter*, the same poem which contains the long passage about Lapland. Alexander continues:

> A storm howled round the dwelling all night, and in the morning the wind was strong from the east: we saw the ice on the Häf broken into huge masses, with icebergs and hummocks on the surface. However, since we

had gone so far there was no retreat, and, having been joined by a Swedish courier who had arrived the night before, we set out over the first field of ice, with two boats and ten hands.

The men were dressed in fur caps and thick drugget: some wore long boots, and the feet of the others were cased in seal-skins. The baggage, a compass, and some frozen meat were placed in the boats, in one of which the corpulent courier fixed himself, armed with a bottle of Cogniac to keep up his courage. The masts of the boats were then stepped, the sails set, an oar rigged across the gunwales of each, by which a couple of hands kept them upright on their keels, two others dragged them by ropes fastened to the cut-water, and a third went in advance with a boat-hook, to try the strength of the ice. With a pair of skates on my feet we hurried onwards, and, at the first open basin we came to the boats were launched, and we pulled over to the next floe.

I had not been long enjoying the pleasure of skating when I fell through a hole, and the party gave me up for lost: however, I scrambled out, and became at once a glittering sheet of ice: but as I stripped instantly and put on other clothes, I sustained no injury; and we continued all day long alternately dragging the boats over the ice, (which in many places was frozen in large waves,) and crossing the open canals and basins by rowing and sailing.

The arrival of the party on the Swedish shore is described like the conclusion of a particularly daring and exciting boy-scout adventure. Indeed, the tone of some of Alexander's writing leads me to wonder if the sub-genre of hyperborean writing was now so established that the heroic could modulate into the mock-heroic:

With a few more accidents in falling through the thin ice, and getting our fingers frozen for a time during a snowstorm, at last, when it was becoming dusk, and after we had been twelve hours on our legs, we descried the pine-covered and rocky shore of Sweden; and singing inspirational airs, we dragged the boats at a run towards the lights of Grisselham, and were congratulated on our escape from the perils of the Häf.

Captain Charles Colville Frankland

Little is known about the career of the next nautical visitor to Finland. According to the naval records Frankland was made Commander in 1825 and Captain not until 1841. What is certain is that by the time he set off for Russia in 1830 he was a hardened explorer, who had recently published *Travels to and from Constantinople* (1829). In that book he praised a way of life and of travelling which must have been very markedly different to the disciplines of the navy:

> The charm of the vagrant kind of life which I led for some weeks in Syria, is inconceivable; its constant variety, its perfect independence, the excitement of difficulty, the apprehension of danger, were so many powerful but agreeable stimulants. My wants were but few and easily supplied; my bed was the ground, my covering a cloak, and my canopy the heavens.

One of the few places where his name can now be found is in the annals of the Long Riders' Guild, dedicated to those, dead as well as living, who have been notable equestrian explorers. One would hardly guess this from the account of his Baltic journey; here he was looking for a new experience. In the Dedication to *Narrative of a Visit to the Courts of Russia and Sweden* (1832) he wrote that he hoped 'to convey . . . a general idea of the society of the North, and of the sort of life that a well-introduced stranger leads at Petersburgh and Moscow'. No sleeping under the stars on this journey! Indeed, his most recurrent concern, at least in the Finnish part of his narrative, is how he got swindled by innkeepers and cheated by money-changers. Another theme is his criticism of the incompetent navigation he was subjected to. He had berated the 'negligence and carelessness of the *steam seamen*' during the passage from England to Hamburg, and his criticisms resumed in his account of the ten days it took by sailing boat from Stockholm to Turku.

Frankland is much more forthcoming in his observations about Sweden than about Finland. He remarks on the incivility of the Swedes: the country itself was 'uncivilised', the post houses 'execrable', and their masters 'boorish and stupid'. He was at least satisfied with his audience with the king: 'His Majesty seems a very unaffected, modest man, speaking of himself with the greatest possible humility.'

With his companion Oakes he embarked on the packet to Turku on 10 September 1830. The weather was first too calm, and then too stormy for them to make progress: 'the Finns,' he wrote, 'are not sufficiently good seamen to venture outside in strong weather and contrary winds.' For the first few days the travellers kept themselves and the other passengers entertained with various games and charades, but as time went by, and supplies ran short, he grew increasingly irritated:

> . . . so improvident are these Finns, and so indolent, that we actually lay four days at Robinson Crusoe's Island [Frankland's nickname], the skipper doing nothing, knowing that his stock of water and provision must soon run out, and not making the slightest exertion to replenish his stores! One would not have believed in such stupidity had one not seen it.

On 18 September they finally got going again, but not for long; when the ship did eventually weigh anchor

it was in vain; we ran ashore four times, in a great degree owing to the awkwardness of the Finns, who have
no idea of the mechanical action of either rudder or
sails.

When the boat was finally tied up the passengers 'went
ashore, and dined at a fisher's cottage upon potatoes and
fish'. As they embarked in the evening, a boat 'with three
savage-looking Russians (one of whom had a long beard,)
came on board to sell brandy'.

Frankland's journal succinctly summarises the end of the
voyage:

> Sept. 19. – At daylight, wind south-west. Weighed and
> made sail, God be praised! for Abo. Jib-topsail, square-
> sail, ring-tail, and water-sail, all set. We ran rapidly
> through the islands.

They arrived after ten days at sea, and 'went to the *Société-
haus,* where we found tolerable accommodation in point of
lodging'. He concluded his entry for the day at midnight:
'Beds pretty good, with dry sheets.'

His criticisms of Baltic seamanship are, like Jones's, very
surprising in light of the long history and great fame of Nor-
dic sailors. In Turku it was the military scene which met his
critical eye:

> There are about 400 infantry here of the twenty-third
> regiment. The soldiers on duty are clean and well-
> clothed, but those off duty, in their long brown drug-
> get great coats, look more like itinerant tinkers than
> soldiers.

Later, on Suomenlinna, he made similar observations about
the 'Russian soldiery'.

Turku was in better order than might have been expected so soon after the fire, with a reported population of 14,000:

> In spite of its recent calamity, it seems, however, to be recovering, and the stroke of a hammer, the sound of the saw and the axe, the explosion of the stone quarry, echo in all directions.

He was puzzled by the fact that the town was 'reconstructing in wood, as it if had never been prey to the devouring element of fire, while immense quarries of fine granite surround it on every side'. They visited the cathedral, which had 'suffered from the dreadful conflagration of 1827. They are now occupied in rebuilding the top of the main tower, which is of enormous height.'

'The theatre of Abo is under the same roof with the *Société-haus*,' wrote Frankland. Åsa Ringbom has described this building, with its public rooms, and its neo-classical façade overlooking the river Aura:

> The upper floor was dominated by a large central assembly hall placed behind the vaulted windows of the main façade. The hall was flanked on either side by chambers for ladies and gentlemen and was furnished by wooden benches along the walls. A music gallery dominated the back wall and painted garlands decorated the inner walls of the room.

Frankland and Oakes spent some of the next evening there, unimpressed, it seems, with either the grandeur of this assembly hall or with the play:

> The performance was bad enough, but better than I could have expected in such a place, and with such heterogeneous materials. The *corps dramatique* is German, that of Monsieur et Madame Schultz. Madame

Schultz is a very fine woman. The tenor was a Jew, and execrably flat; the woman was tolerable: the devil did not sing – I suppose his satanic majesty was ill.

They left Turku the next morning 'at thirty minutes past nine, after being cheated by the inn-keeper at the *Société-haus*' and set off for St Petersburg; the account of the journey is, unfortunately, very little more than a list of the post house stops (e.g. Salo; 'corn and a river'). Svenskby alone comes in for any detailed comment:

Good post-house, civil people, the post-master speaking German, and making brandy (not strong enough for [their guide] Jonas's palate). Supper upon black cock and fresh eggs, bread and excellent butter. Clean beds: turn in.

Helsinki was the first place that he stopped:

Sept. 23 – I arose early, and sallied out to look at the city. It indeed surpasses any expectation I had previously formed: it is the most beautiful and the most interesting new city I ever beheld. The Russian Emperor, the Trajan of the North, might say with the Roman, that he found it a pack of wooden huts, and left it a city of palaces.

Frankland's interest was, naturally, in the ships, and also in the decayed dock on Suomenlinna. The life of the city did not impress him; all he mentions is that they 'went to see a conjuror with learned dogs'. He sums up Helsinki society very abruptly: 'Little beauty, and less fashion.'

The only occasion when he does more than list stopping places on his way to St Petersburg is when he describes an accident on the road. There are few travellers from this era who did not comment on the dare-devil practices of the drivers (very often young boys), who went at top speed from post to post. Breakdowns were more commonly described than accidents, perhaps because only survivors left accounts.

At ten wersts from Holmgard, charging *à la Finnoise* down a hill in the dark, we came violently in contact with a rock; the shock was enough to have broken any but a very strongly-built carriage into a thousand pieces. However, thus far all was safe; but upon breasting a hill just in our front, the horses jibbed, and running the britchkha violently against (as I believe) the same rock, turned us completely over, threw the postboy into the woods, and Jonas upon the rocks. We scrambled out to pick him up: he lay groaning, and vowing that his leg was broken. This was a little *ruse* on his part, to distract our attention from the fractured carriage to his limb. Fortunately, no bones were broken. After having dispatched the postboy on one of his own horses to the next post for assistance, we succeeded in lighting one of the lamps by means of phosphoric matches, and examined the state of the vehicle. No injury was sustained, save the staving in of the calèche, and the fracture of the strap which binds the fore train to the hinder, near the driving-bolt (or maschio), and one lamp. Oakes now mounted upon one of the remaining bare-backed horses, and went back to Holmgard for aid, while I stayed watching the carriage and encouraging Jonas, whose fall (more like that of Vulcan than Phaëton) was likely to produce sad consequences to his peripatetics. 'Oh!' said he, 'that I should ever have come to this; I that have driven to Torneo and to Drontheim twenty times with Englishmen, and never was upset before. Oh the pretty travelling carriage! that has come so many hundred miles safely, and is now broken to pieces!' &c.&c. 'Better,' said I, 'Jonas, that the carriage should be broken than your neck.' 'Oh no!' said he, 'I had rather die a hundred times over than that this should happen.'

Help finally arrived from Holmgård, the carriage was re- trieved and righted, and they arrived at their next post, Phytää, at midnight to find 'only one bed, and no provi- sions'.

Frankland was not entirely blind to his surroundings; he goes so far as to mention briefly that the distant view of Hamina 'is beautiful, with river or arm of the sea, green cupolas, and spires'. At Pyterlahti too 'the roads were beau- tiful' but the

people extremely savage, and long-bearded, drunken, poor, and miserably lodged. Near this are the famous granite quarries, but the road to them is so execrable, that I did not wish to trust my already shaken vehicle upon it.

Two days later he and his vehicle arrived at the 'beautiful town' of Vyborg.

Charles Boileau Elliott

On the title-page of his *Letters from the North of Europe* (1832) Elliott is described as 'of the Bengali Civil Service, of Queen's [*sic*] College Cambridge, and Member of the Royal Geographical Society'. Each of these designations is reflected in the letters which make up his book. He writes as a seasoned traveller, praising the mountainous prospects in Norway with knowledgeable comparisons to the Alps and the Himalayas. He makes a scholarly distinction between facts, which are 'recorded with fidelity' and his opinions, which 'are not entitled to be received with equal confidence'. He had done some preparation for his journey north, having read, at least, the *Travels* of Captain Jones and of Brooke.

Elliott travelled through Finland in the late summer of 1830; his route had been through Holland to Copenhagen, via Gothenburg to Christiana (Oslo) and Bergen, crossing Sweden via Carlstad and Örebro to Stockholm. He took the usual sea route 'on a Finnish packet' to Turku. This was possibly a steam packet, since the journey took only about forty-eight hours. He gives virtually no account of it; presumably this was a rare instance of a calm sea and a prosperous voyage on the Gulf. The only surprise was a pleasant one: having heard much of 'the rigidity of the Russian custom and police', he found that

> instead of a search, I was invited, with other passengers, to take coffee on shore with the superintending officer; and had the opportunity of observing the manners of a Finnish family.

He gives virtually no details of the journey across Finland on the usual route to St Petersburg. In Turku, at the invitation of the Swedish consul-general, he 'joined his family circle in the evening in order to see something of Finnish manners. Such opportunities are not to be lost . . .' Unfortunately for us they are lost, since he records nothing at all about the occasion, except that the consul gave him 'much information'. He made only one new addition to the list of what the British had seen in Turku:

> There is a floating market here, like that of Stockholm, for the sale of vegetables. The women stand knee-deep in water; and a little parapet, raised on the bed of the river, serves to secure the market from being carried away by the stream, while it affords a dry walk for the customers.

Elliott 'joined purses' with an English fellow-traveller in Turku, and they bought a calèche; 'a miserable conveyance,' he wrote, 'and the repairs have given us much trouble'. He was one of many travellers to have been caught out like this; a few years later Murray's *Guide* would strongly advise buying a carriage in Stockholm, and shipping it across. In it their journey began:

> The road is good; and the country flat, like Sweden, but of a wilder character; the foreground being chiefly rocky, with forests in the distance. The horses are small. They go at a full gallop; and the velocity with which a carriage generally moves down-hill cannot fail to try the nerves. We hired a coachman for five pounds from Abo to St Petersburg. He can talk only the language of the country; and when my companion calls out to him, which he does repeatedly, and always with increased energy, to drive slower, the man conceives that we are

urging him to greater speed, and flogs the horses more and more, till the weak fabric of the carriage swings fearfully from side to side. However, with or without danger, we have been making rapid progress, and as nothing is to be gained by delay, that is what we desire. Travelling in Finland is superior to, and cheaper than, that of any country in the world.

In Turku he had stayed at 'La Société', now becoming the inn of choice for travellers, but in Helsinki, where they spent a night, they were 'conducted to an indefinite sort of establishment, half private and half coffee-house, where little comfort [was] to be found'. He admired the public buildings which were going up, and wrote that the town 'will soon rank among the finest of the northern capitals'. From Helsinki they made for Hamina, which was 'still sadly desolate, only a part having been rebuilt' after the fire. They travelled as fast as they could until they arrived at Vyborg:

> An excellent inn, the only good one I have seen since leaving Hamburg, is in the hands of a plausible Italian, who kept us in good-humor while he filled our mouths and picked our pockets.

The carriage, after numerous running repairs, had broken down completely at 'Kyrola', and only prolonged work by 'a blacksmith and carpenter truly oriental' got it back on the road to convey the travellers to the Russian border at Rajajoki. After leaving Finland Elliott continued to St Petersburg and Moscow, later returning to England by way of Riga and Prussia. The steamer crossing from Hamburg he considered the most dangerous experience not only of this expedition but of his life.

Elliott's style is noticeably different from that of Jones and Alexander. As befits a Cambridge man, he is a literary writer, with an instinctive range of classical reference, and he has an eye for the picturesque. He often writes more like a novelist than a geographer, and his vocabulary is at times reminiscent even of Jane Austen's: the view from the observatory hill in Turku, for example, is 'such a one as satisfies at first sight'. He even shares her Johnsonian taste for moral generalisation:

> It is a happy circumstance that man is so constituted that the only charm required to attach him to any country is that it should be his own. The Fins would not exchange their country and their servitude for the freedom of England, much less for the romantic hills of Norway or of Switzerland. Their patriotism has been the theme of admiration among all nations and all ages.

Another instance of Elliott's refinement is that, of the many travellers who had quoted or alluded to the stark account of the Fenni given by Tacitus, he alone continues the quotation:

> Yet even this way of life is in their estimation happier than groaning over the plough, toiling in the erection of houses; subjecting their own fortunes and those of others to the agitation of alternate hope and fear. Secure against men, secure against the gods, they have attained that most difficult point, not to need even a wish.

Particularly distinctive is the way in which Elliott is at every stage of his journey reminded of India. At times it sounds as it he is embodying the notion, which Thomas Love Peacock brought to perfection in his *Crotchet Castle* (1831), of characters completely dominated by a single fixed idea. In northern Norway he had fancied that the peasants hay-making could have been acting out a scene from Bengal; in Finland, he wrote, 'I could fancy myself in Asia', and the country surrounding Turku 'is a mass of barren granite, resembling the environs of Delhi'. Elliott justifies these allusions as the hallmark of 'that comparative study of countries and their productions [which] falls immediately within the province of a traveller'. This is a serious claim, and Elliott stands out among all these early travellers as an observer who assesses what he describes in Finland by placing it in wider contexts. A good example is his vivid description of the physical appearance of the Finns:

> The men could not possibly be mistaken for civilized beings. The hair is sometimes in youth bright auburn, and generally in maturer years of a light brown color; but always disgustingly dirty. Here, as in Scandinavia, it seldom, even in age, falls off. The men wear it quite covering the ears, and as long in front, but shaved off the back of the head. Their necks are left bare, and their faces are untonsured. Less pleasing objects are not often presented to the eye. The women wear their hair fastened at the top in a conical roll, sometimes ornamented with a piece of colored cloth.

This could have been written by any one of half-a-dozen travellers of the period, but Elliott follows his unflattering description with an interpretative paragraph, which displays also an impressive range of tonsorial knowledge:

> It is curious to observe the various modes which nations have adopted of dressing the hair. The Saracens wore it long, having 'faces as the faces of men (that is, unshaven,) and hair as the hair of women'. A Chinaman cuts the hair off the rest of the head, but wears it on the scalp, where it is cherished till it will form three queues, substantially plaited and reaching to the

ground. The Hindoo holds only one queue orthodox, and that a small one, by which he hopes to be dragged up into heaven. The rest of the head is submitted to a weekly tonsure. A Catholic priest, on the other hand, shaves only the little spot on the crown where the Hindoo allows the hair to grow. The Mussulman, inverting the Russian mode, and adopting a style peculiar to himself, shaves the upper half of the head and preserves a semi-circular tuft of hair behind.

Elliott is an attractive version of the typical English gentleman of the time: elegant, educated and reflective, but neither very curious nor especially observant. At times he is rather too delicate to face the less polished manifestations of the North. He is not the only Englishman to have flinched at schnapps:

A fashion prevails throughout the North of taking a glass of spirits with anchovies, or something equally piquant, to stimulate the appetite before entering the dining-room. This is a vile system, equally bad in theory and practice.

His embarrassment when his Finnish companion in Turku kisses him goodbye is a nice example of well-bred English reticence:

The worthy *camero,* our fellow-passenger from Stockholm, left Abo an hour or two before us. I had won his affection by telling stories in a jargon of German and Swedish, mixed up with French, to his little girl. Accordingly, he came to me in the yard of the inn, and, taking off his hat, made a profound bow, which I returned in kind and courtesy. Approaching nearer, he took my hand and uttered sundry incomprehensible words. To these I replied by bows. A further approximation of his face to mine terminated in a salute of my right cheek, and then the left, which astonished me not a little. Perhaps I felt less grateful than in duty bound; for the good man's chin, not 'newly reaped,'

    'Was like a stubble field at harvest-home.'

and wounded me sensibly! I had not anticipated such a welcome to Finland.

John Barrow

The author of *Excursions in the North of Europe,* published in 1834, appears on the title-page as 'John Barrow, Junr.'. Barrow's father was a notable traveller and author, and among many achievements as Second Secretary to the Admiralty for forty years, promoted voyages of discovery to the Arctic; the Barrow Strait in the Canadian Arctic is named after him. He was a prolific contributor to *The Quarterly Review*, and perhaps had a hand in the favourable review of his son's book.

The younger Barrow followed his father into the Admiralty, and was 'equally active in geographical and Royal Society circles', publishing in all ten volumes of travels. His first 'excursion' was in 1830 to St Petersburg and Moscow via Hamburg and Lübeck, returning through Finland and Denmark; the second was to Denmark and Norway in 1833. Each of the journeys took about two months, and both were made with a companion, Mr Rouse. 'Our movements,' he writes in his Preface, 'were guided by the spur of the moment, without preparation or premeditated design.'

Barrow and Rouse embarked at London on 26 June 1830 for Hamburg. After sightseeing there they took the 'execrable road to Lubeck', and then a second steamer direct to Kronstadt. They made the journey from Petersburg to Moscow and back again, and on 31 August set off to travel through Finland to Stockholm. They bought a basket-work carriage, long enough to permit lying full-length, which, with a straw mattress and various cushions, 'caused the journey as far as Abo to be performed with every possible degree of ease and comfort'. For most of the way the road 'was kept in beautiful order; not a hollow or rut of any description', and they accomplished the 418-mile journey in four days:

> The posting is remarkably cheap, averaging from about three halfpence to two pence a mile for each horse. Our light wagon hurried along at a great rate, sometimes with a rapidity which rendered it, as we thought, dangerous: on one occasion, in particular, we were driven by a little boy not more than eleven or twelve years old, who drove the poor horses at a full gallop for a whole stage over a road which twisted and turned among rocks in every possible direction. We had to pass several small wooden bridges, over brooks rippling down the valleys, and here our young driver seemed to take tremendous delight in galloping at a tremendous rate down the hill and across these bridges, by which such an impetus was given to the vehicle that we were at the top of the next on the other side in a moment.

On his four-day journey he has little more to remark of 'the face of the country' than that 'it is of a pleasing character'. They travelled day and night because they could not contemplate sleeping at a post-station:

> The post stations at the villages, without one exception, are miserable hovels, and totally unfit for any traveller to think of sleeping in. Nothing could exceed the wretched and filthy state of the interior of some of these houses, which are only entered for the purposes of writing one's names in the book kept at each station.

As if this were not bad enough, they failed to find anything fit to eat or drink:

As we proceeded, the surface became undulated by hill and dale, both clothed with forests of pine trees, but the eye was occasionally greeted by the sight of a beautiful lake, which would now and then agreeably burst upon the view; but there did not appear to be much ground under tillage. That this part of Finland was but little cultivated was too evident, from the scanty and bad quality of the subsistence to be met with in all the villages through which we passed, and in which we were rarely able to procure any other species of provisions than the coarsest brown bread, baked as hard as a sailor's biscuit, or burnt rather to a cinder, which in appearance it pretty much resembled. Add to this a little fish, dried or salted, sour cream, and some-times, though not always, salted butter – and you have the sum total of what may be expected in a Finnish vil-lage. Fortunately we had been informed of this scarcity before starting, and had laid in a tolerably good stock of tongues, chickens, and other good things, together with a small supply of eau de vie, which we thought would have been sufficient, with the addition of any other beverage we might chance to meet with; but in this we were disappointed; we found nothing whatever but the ardent spirit called *Votki:* so that when our little stock of brandy was exhausted, we had to resort to this native liquor, which we had heard much abused and execrated as a most villainous beverage, but which we did not find to deserve such a character. The flavour is more that of whiskey than any other spirit, is exceed-ingly fiery, but, when mixed with hot water and sugar, is by no means unpleasant.

They had engaged a servant in St Petersburg, to travel with them as interpreter; we learn a little from Barrow about their relationship as he lifts just a corner of the veil which usually excludes servants from the traveller's narrative. The servants must have have had a harder time than any of the travellers who employed them, but none of them has told his tale:

> To this man, on our arrival at Abo, we paid one hundred roubles for his services. In a written agreement which had been drawn up and signed by him to prevent misunderstanding, a plan I cannot too strongly recommend, it was mentioned that he was to provide his own food, which was found to be a very necessary precaution, as every traveller on this road is obliged to carry his own provisions with him. As far as we were enabled, however, to do so, we allowed him to partake of our fare; but this was, of course, meant and received as an indulgence. We had every reason to be perfectly satisfied with his conduct on all occasions; and though we travelled three nights out of the four that were spent on the road, he never made the slightest complaint, nor appeared to be the least displeased or out of humour, which he certainly had reason to be, had he thought fit to show it.

Barrow was fleetingly impressed by Vyborg and by Hamina, where 'we passed along a street that might be called handsome in any country'. The only other towns Barrow mentions are Loviisa, 'a pretty little town enough', and Helsinki, 'the largest and handsomest of any that we passed'. Neither place detained them; all sightseeing gave way to the rush for Turku:

> It was about two o'clock in the morning when we drove into the large court-yard of the inn at Abo, and all was still and silent as the grave. In vain did we knock at

every door, and tap at every window within our reach: not a soul appeared to be in existence. Fatigued with a long journey, and sadly disappointed with the prospect of sleeping in the open air, for I had long set my mind on a comfortable rest, I sauntered up and down the yard in a fit of melancholy, and heartily wished myself either at home, or again at Petersburg. I was, however, suddenly aroused from my despondency by our courier, who had spied out a couple of legs dangling from a hay-loft, and with the utmost difficult succeeded in waking the owner of them, and in the course of an hour or more we were accommodated with a room, having a couple of sofas, on which we slept soundly.

In contrast to their non-stop dash across Finland, they had to wait in Turku for a favourable wind. As a consequence Barrow gives quite a detailed account of the city. In the few years since the visits of Alexander and Frankland the rebuilding had continued apace:

Abo appeared to be by far the most busy place we had touched at since leaving Petersburg – all was life and animation. In the upper part of the town, workmen were busily employed in blasting the rocks to obtain building materials and for forming a new road, and houses were to be seen in progress in every direction. The blows of the hammers, which commenced at a very early hour of the day and lasted till dusk, reminded me of the noise in a dock-yard, when the men are employed on ships on the stocks.

They evidently stayed in the 'Society House', the same inn that Frankland had described a few years earlier, and like him, they found their chief entertainment in Turku at the theatre:

We found ourselves comfortable enough lodged at the inn. Part of its establishment was a small theatre, the only one, I believe, at Abo, which occupied the upper story of the building. One performance took place during our residence at the inn at which we, as a matter of course, did not fail to be present. The audience were seated on benches arranged in a similar manner to those in the pit of any other theatre, and the space for these benches was divided into three parts, the first, and that nearest the stage, being the most select, and consequently of the highest price, answered to the boxes in our own theatres, – the second division to the pit, and the third to the gallery. The theatre was well attended; that is to say, being calculated to hold about 200 persons, there could not have been less than 150 present. The performance was carried on with great spirit, and appeared to give much satisfaction to those of the audience who understood it, which did not include ourselves. As far as I could make out the play, it appeared to me that all the jokes turned upon our own countrymen. The principal character was an Englishman, but his representative was as unlike one as is possible to conceive; he was supposed to be in love with some fair damsel who rejected his addresses. He was on his knees repeatedly before her, which greatly amused the company; but at last finding that he was unable to make any impression on the cruel lady, and despairing of ever gaining her affections, he threatened to destroy himself, and made preparations accordingly, which set the whole audience in a roar of laughter. Several eyes were turned towards us during the performance, and we made a point of laughing at every joke, though it was no difficult matter to do so at such an absurd representation of

John Bull. This theatre proved a great source of amusement to us during our detention by a foul wind, for having seen all the was worth seeing, we were much at a loss to pass the four days we were detained at Abo, one of which was amply sufficient to satisfy curiosity. The stage-manager, or the superintendent of the *corps dramatique*, was one of the most lively, good natured men I have ever met with, and spoke French fluently. He resided in the hotel, and we soon became excellent friends, so much so, that he allowed us to attend the rehearsals in the mornings whenever we pleased. By candle-light the heroes and heroines looked tolerably decent and respectable, but when we saw them by day-light it would be impossible to imagine a more ill-favoured set, not even in the booths of a country fair in England, or at St. Bartholomew.

On the night of the representation, there were many well-dressed ladies present, and amongst them a very tolerable share of beauty. Indeed, the audience was chiefly composed of females. There were two very smart-looking young ladies who particularly caught our attention, and whom we considered as the prettiest girls present. These we afterwards discovered were the daughters of our landlord, but they kept themselves so closely shut up that we were not fortunate enough to get one glimpse of them again during our stay in the same house.

After some days the wind still had not changed, so the boat was towed out of the harbour by the crew, and tacking its way towards Åland, made the journey in four days, despite being grounded briefly. They found plenty of company to enliven the time:

Our fellow-voyagers at the fore part of the vessel were a merry set of people, and seemed to be at no loss in finding amusement among themselves. One evening, while becalmed among the islands, the female part of these joyous passengers took it into their heads to act a play – something, probably, of their own extemporaneous invention; but whatever it was, it had the effect of making both themselves and their audience laugh immoderately; and though we, in the after part of the vessel, understood nothing of the matter, we found their merriment was catching, and were obliged to join in the laugh. The passengers, also, from their different dresses and manners, afforded us a source of amusement in our tardy progress. One of the smartest-looking was a gentleman dressed in a light blue frock-coat, buttoned closely up to the throat, whom I conjectured, from his appearance, to be a Prussian officer of some distinction, but he turned out to be a printer at Stockholm. An old woman, who could not have been far short of seventy, particularly attracted our notice in the course of the voyage from her extraordinary activity: indeed, she seemed nearly as much at home, with regard to her knowledge of the ropes, as any of the sailors, and constantly lent a hand in tacking the vessel.

Barrow was one of the last travellers to cross to Stockholm by sailing boat, and certainly the last Englishman, of many, to describe the route. The journey between Turku and Stockholm would never be the same again, as Barrow anticipates:

We were informed, that at one time a steam-boat used to run between Abo and Stockholm, but that, unfortunately, they contrived to get her on shore last year among some the numberless rocks or shoals, when she received so much damage as to be rendered totally unfit for further service without a very expensive repair; and as we heard nothing of her either at Abo or Stockholm, I conclude the proprietors thought it the most prudent step to break her up: it was said, however, that preparations were making to replace her by another, intended to start on fixed days, which, across this gulf in particular, must prove to be of the greatest convenience to travellers.

John Barrow is a transitional figure in the developing history of travelling in Finland. He arrived by steamer, but left by sailing boat; once in Finland he travelled by traditional means, in his own carriage, using post horses. Within a few years steamers plying on the Baltic would completely change the face of travel, at least during the summer months.

Charlotte Disbrowe and
the Marchioness of Westminster

It is not until the late 1820s that women leave any record of travelling in Finland; oddly enough, both of the women who did travel at this time waited more than fifty years before they published their accounts. We know that Paterson's wife travelled with her husband on some of his journeys, but more typically travellers were glad that their womenfolk had been spared such hardships.

Charlotte Disbrowe's *Original Letters from Russia* were published in 1878 by the Ladies' Printing Press, but relates to the years 1825–8, when she was living with her father, the 'Minister Plenipotentiary at the Court of St. Petersburg'. Like Paterson, and several travellers of the following decades, she was permanently resident in St Petersburg, and able to take short trips to Finland. There is no other similarity to Paterson, as her letter reveals: he was a dour Congregationalist minister, whereas she has very much the voice and vocabulary of one of Jane Austen's young chatterboxes. The following letter could easily be one of the Musgrove girls in *Persuasion* describing her jaunt to Lyme Regis:

> (St. P.) 22nd August,
> 4th September, I believe, 1825.
> Our little trip into Finland succeeded famously. I was very vexed at undertaking it without Papa, as we had promised to wait for him, and I had refused to join another party on purpose that we might go together, but Mr. Disbrowe was afraid Baron Nicolaï might be gone, and that the weather would prevent our going later. So off we set, accompanied by General Dornberg,

the Hanoverian Minister, a most agreeable elderly person. Our attelage beat anything I saw during the whole course of my travels. Four little atoms of horses abreast, driven by our own coachman, and two leaders ridden by a postilion with a flowing mane, and generally in his shirt, tho' sometimes we were favoured with a coat of sheepskin, the wool inside. We went at an amazing pace, and always full gallop up hill, which discomposed Parker's and my nerves at first most amazingly; however, we met with no accident. The greater part of Finland seems composed of granite, so that the roads were hard and smooth as tables, (for want of a better comparison) and the only difficulty was to wind safely between the enormous masses of rock thro' which the road is cut. We were disappointed with the cataract of Imatta, and yet it certainly is a fine sight to see a broad river forcing its way through a narrow passage of steep rocks. However, a cascade is so much more picturesque that I suspect that was the cause of our disappointment, and we could not help comparing this torrent, to Schaffhausen, which tho' not as great a body of water, makes almost as much fuss, and forms a prettier picture. Our visit to the Baron's at Mon Repos, close to Wyborg, was very pleasant; his garden is one of the lions of the country, it is on the sea-shore, and abounds in masses of the granite, which offers plenty of scope for varying the scenery, and he has taken wonderful advantage of it, by ornamenting it with temples, towers, shrubberies, pillars, etc., etc. On one promontory he has built a gothic castle, dedicated to the memory of his parents; had permission to have the ground consecrated, and made it a family burial place. His father and mother and two children are already interred there, and the vault for his wife, who died at Copenhagen about a year-and-a-half ago, is nearly finished. I should not like such an arrangement in my garden at all, it would make me melancholy.

Yesterday I had the felicity of unpacking my Parisian boxes . . .

Miss Disbrowe's taste is beyond reproach; it would not be very long before Imatra was presenting a much prettier picture, with a viewing tower, if not a temple.

This volume concludes with some very brief extracts from the diary of a young lady, travelling with her husband, Viscount Belgrave. She refers to him as Belgrave throughout; he later became the second Marquess of Westminster. The trip took place in 1827, but the *Diary* was not published until 1879. In her Preface the Marchioness wrote:

the way of travelling at that time, fifty-two years ago, may be amusing when contrasting with the present easy and rapid means of transport in distant countries.

This is certainly true, but I have put this writer a little out of place in my chronology because she represents unequivocally the end of the age of the pioneering traveller. All the previous authors presented here have been, in some senses, adventurers. The Marchioness is the first of the bored travellers, for whom scenes are either 'delightful' or 'charming'. In Stockholm she condescended to the Queen of Sweden:

The Queen is the most good-natured creature possible, and was very kind to us, admiring my dress and my hair, which certainly showed good taste.

It was hardly likely that, after patronising Stockholm, she would have any significant or valuable impressions of Finland, nor did she. She 'found the packet very comfortable':

Nothing could be more delightful than the whole of the passage. Towards evening we had our first sight of Abo, which looked extremely pretty at the end of an intricate bay; a sort of road is marked out in the water with piles of wood, and called 'the Channel'. It leads straight up to the town, and you sail a considerable way up a line of river or canal with houses on each side, very like a Dutch town.

We arrived at seven, and disembarked soon after with perfect ease, close to the inn where we intended to lodge; both the carriages were got out before nine, and we found tolerable rooms at 'La Société'. After we had settled ourselves in them, we went out for a walk, and by means of wooden steps mounted a high hill over-hanging the town, and crowned by the Observatory. Though it was nearly dark, the view over the town was very fine, and we found Abo much more considerable and much handsomer than we had had expected.

She and the Viscount continued to Helsinki, to

Mademoiselle Washlund's hotel, where we found toler-able rooms. We went out to walk in the town, which is beautiful, very clean-looking with very handsome houses and a fine *Place*.

With the Marchioness of Westminster the age of the tour-ist has unmistakably begun.

Epilogue

By the late 1820s British travel in Finland had changed almost beyond recognition, and the changes would continue during the rest of the century. During the 1820s many developments were becoming evident: the intermittent appearance of steamers on the Gulf of Bothnia, the resort of travellers to an inn in Turku variously described as 'the Societat', the 'Society house', and 'La Société', and the arrival of British ladies on the Finnish scene. By the end of the century there would be a Societetshuset (Seurahuone) in almost every town, and ladies would be taking summer tours unchaperoned. Already there had been accounts by travellers from different social classes and professions; this trend would continue.

An extraordinary change is that from about 1800 Lapland almost disappears as a destination; with just two enterprising exceptions, it is a century before there is another published account of Finnish Lapland. We have, in addition, seen the end of British accounts of winter travelling; Finland was already being promoted as a summer holiday destination.

There are many reasons, most of them conjectural, for what we see in the following fifty years. This period is really a hiatus between the early, adventurous explorers displayed in this volume, and the full-blown tourists, travelling to Finland from England by luxury steamer. What is obvious is that the extraordinary range of interests which had taken so many curious travellers to Finland in the later eighteenth century had evaporated. The tradition of the Grand Tour, or even its shadows and substitutes, had vanished, and

Oxford and Cambridge were now providing the education which they had in several ways lost sight of in the eighteenth century. There was no more interest in Lapland magic, the vogue of the primitive had run its course, Rousseau had made way for Bentham, and artists had moved on from the picturesque and Romantic. When John Murray published his first *Handbook for Travellers* in 1839 the last 'unvisited corner' of Europe had been mapped, and genuine pioneers, adventurers and natural historians had to go much further afield to get away from beaten tracks.

Appendices

1 Continuation (from pages 8–9) of the Lapland passage
  from James Thomson's *The Seasons*

> Their reindeer form their riches. These their tents,
> Their robes, their beds, and all their homely wealth
> Supply, their wholesome fare, and cheerful cups.
> Obsequious at their call, the docile tribe
> Yield to the sled their necks, and whirl them swift
> O'er hill and dale, heaped into one expanse
> Of marbled snow, or, far as eye can sweep,
> With a blue crust of ice unbounded glazed.
> By dancing meteors then, that ceaseless shake
> A waving blaze refracted o'er the heavens,
> And vivid moons, and stars that keener play
> With doubled lustre from the radiant waste,
> Even in the depth of polar night they find
> A wondrous day – enough to light the chase
> Or guide their daring steps to Finland fairs.
> Wished spring returns; and from the hazy south,
> While dim Aurora slowly moves before,
> The welcome Sun, just verging up at first,
> By small degrees extends the swelling curve;
> Till, seen at last for gay rejoicing months,
> Still round and round his spiral course he winds,
> And, as he nearly dips his flaming orb,
> Wheels up again and re-ascends the sky.
> In that glad season, from the lakes and floods,
> Where pure Niëmi's fairy mountains rise,
> And fringed with roses Tenglio rolls his stream,
> They draw the copious fry. With these at eve
> They cheerful-loaded to their tents repair,
> Where, all day long in useful cares employed,
> Their kind unblemished wives the fire prepare.

Thrice happy race! By poverty secured
From legal plunder and rapacious power,
In whom fell interest never yet has sown
The seeds of vice, whose spotless swains ne'er knew
Injurious deed, nor, blasted by the breath
Of faithless love, their blooming daughters woe.

ll. 851–6

2 Three Lapland poems

From *The Spectator,* No. 336, 19 April 1712:

'A Lapland love-song'

The translator, Ambrose Phillips, explains:
I have ventured to bind it in stricter measures, as being more proper
for our tongue, though perhaps wilder graces may better suit the
genius of the Laponian language.

It will be necessary to imagine that the author of this song, not
having the liberty to visit his mistress at her father's home, was in
hopes of spying her at a distance in her fields.

Thou rising sun, whose gladsome ray
Invites my fair to rural play,
Dispel the mist, and clear the skies,
And bring my Orra to my eyes.

Oh! were I sure my dear to view,
I'd climb that pine-tree's topmost bough,
Aloft in air, that quiv'ring plays,
And round and round for ever gaze.

My Orra Moor, where art thou laid?
What wood conceals my sleeping maid?
Fast by the roots, enrag'd I'd tear
The trees that hide my promised fair.

Oh! could I ride the clouds and skies!
Or on the raven's pinions rise!
Ye storks, ye swans, a moment stay,
And waft a lover on his way.

My bliss too long my bride denies,
Apace the wasting summer flies:
Nor yet the wintry blasts I fear,
Not storms, or night shall keep me here.

What may for strength with steel compare?
Oh! love has fetters stronger far!
By bolts of steel are limbs confined,
But cruel love enchains the mind.

No longer then perplex thy breast,
When thoughts torment, the first are best;
'Tis mad to go; 'tis death to stay;
Away to Orra, haste away.

From *The Spectator*, No. 406, 16 June 1712:

'The Lover addresses his reindeer'

I

Haste my rein-deer, and let us nimbly go
Our am'rous journey through this dreary waste:
Haste my rein-deer! still, still art thou too slow,
Impetuous love demands the lightning's haste.

II

Around us far the rushy moors are spread;
Soon will the sun withdraw his cheerful ray;
Darkling and tir'd we shall the marshes tread,
No lay unsung to cheat the tedious way.

III

The wat'ry length of these unjoyous moors
Does all the flowr'y meadows' pride excel.
Through these I fly to her my soul adores:
Ye flow'ry meadows, empty pride, farewell.

IV

Each moment from the charmer I'm confined,
My breast is tortur'd with impatient fires;
Fly my reindeer, fly swifter than the wind,
Thy tardy feet wing with my fierce desires.

V

Our pleasing toil will soon be then o'erpaid,
And thou in wonder lost, shall view my fair,
Admire each feature of the lovely maid,
Her artless charms, her bloom, her sprightly air.

VI

But lo! with graceful motion there she swims,
Gently removing each ambitious wave;
The crowding waves, transported clasp her limbs;
When, when, oh when? shall I such freedom have!

VII

In vain, ye envious streams, so fast ye flow,
To hide her from her lover's ardent gaze:
From every touch you more transparent grow,
And all reveal'd the beauteous wanton plays.

From Matthew Consett's *Tour* (pp.63–4):

'A Lapland Song'

The Snows are dissolving on Tornea's rude side,
And the Ice of Lulhea flows down the dark tide:
Thy dark stream, Oh Lulhea, flows freely away,
And the Snow-drop unfolds her pale beauties to Day.

Far off the keen terrors of Winter retire,
And the North's dancing Streamers relinquish their fire
The Sun's genial beams swell the bud on the tree,
And Enna chaunts forth her wild warblings with glee.

The Rein-deer, unharness'd in freedom shall play
And safely o'er Odon's steep precipice stray;
The Wolf to the Forest's recesses shall fly,
And howl to the moon as she glides thro' the sky.

The haste, my fair Luah, Oh! haste to the Grove,
And pass the sweet Season in rapture and love;
In Youth let our bosoms in Extacy grow
For the winter of Life ne'er a transport can know.

3 The Great Coastal Road, and the post route to Sweden

From Captain Charles Colville Frankland, RN, *Narrative of a Visit to the Courts of Russia and Sweden, in the Years 1830 and 1832* (1832), Vol. I, 398–9. This list of stopping places is the most comprehensive which I have found, but is not definitive. I have not attempted to identify all the places mentioned; a few still keep these Swedish names. On the evidence of this list, and the various accounts given by travellers, one may say confidently that the Great Coastal Road was not great, not always coastal, and not always even a road. (A Swedish mile is ten kilometres, and a Russian verst just over one kilometre.)

ROUTE FROM ABO, IN FINLAND, TO PETERSBURGH.

Distance in Swedish miles

Abo – Tolerable Inn at the Society House
1¾ to Rungo (Stadt gelt)
1½ Vista
1¾ Hăndălă
1 Salo
1⅞ Hämenkyla
1¾ Svenskby (Good post-house, and clean)
2 Björsby
1¾ Mjölbolstadt
1½ Bolstadt
2 Qvis
1⅝ Remböle
1½ Grann
1½ Helsingfors (tolerable inn sur la Place)
1½ Henricksdal (Stadt gelt)
1¾ Sibbo
1¼ Veikaski
1¼ Borgo (Tolerable inn, Madame Lotta's)
1 Illby
1 5/16 Forssby
1½ Perno
1⅜ Lovisa (First Russ station)

Distance in Wersts

10⅝ Holmgard

16¼ Pyttis (New post-house)

20   Fredrickshamm (Tolerable post-house)

17   Grãnvick

17   Pyterlax (Visit stone quarries)

16   Urpala

16½ Săckjărvi

15   Nisalax (Good post-house)

15½ Wiborg (Good inn, kept by an Italian: here get
         Padarosjna and viser passport)

18   Lillpero

17   Hotacka

13   Kyrălă

13   Pampala (Good post house)

13   Kivinebb

13   Rajajoki

12   Baloastraff (Customs)

15   Dranischnikoff

18½ St. Petersburgh.

In Finland the price of posting is 6 copecks per horse per verst, or 60 copecks the Swedish mile, excepting upon leaving towns, when, as in Sweden, the price is double. Trinkgelt from 20 to 30 kopecks a station. Remember at Abo or at Helsingfors to get plenty of small Finnish notes to pay the postilions with.

George Green, *An Original Journal from London to St Petersburg* (1813), 160–1, gives the post houses north of Turku, and some details of the 'first arm' of the Gulf crossing (all distances in Swedish miles):

2¼ Mases Namini

1½ Menkily

2¼ Laites

2¼ Hemoisi

1¾ Helsinge

From Helsinge, in winter, your carriages and yourself are drawn over the first arm of the Gulph to the first island called Warsala, by men; in summer both are transported by boat. In the first mode you must make the best bargain you can to get from island to island; but in the latter season there is fixed price by order of government, printed in the title-page of all the post-books. which at every post-house are presented to you to sign; and if you have reason to insert any complaint, these books are sent every month to the governor of the province . . .

Passage of the Islands
Helsing to Warsala	$1\frac{1}{3}$
Warsala to Brando	$2\frac{1}{2}$
Wargata	1
Skorpas	$1\frac{1}{2}$
Harralsby	$1\frac{1}{2}$
Enkarby	$1\frac{1}{2}$
Morby	$1\frac{1}{4}$
Echerv	7
Here the Islands end.	
Griselham by sea	7

4 Clarke's 'General Statement of Contents'

(Volume IX) Chapter IX

FROM TORNEÅ, TO THE MOUTH OF THE MUONIO RIVER

Preparations for an Expedition beyond the Arctic Circle – Lapland Beds – The Party leave Torneå – Salmon Fishery – Falls of the Lapland Rivers – Manner of passing them – Incipient Trap – Frankilä – Antient mode of covering the head – Dr. Deutsch – Carl Gustaf – Steam Baths – Korpikylä – Cataract of Matka Koski – Primæval Mill – Beverage of the Laplanders – Rubus Chamæmorus – Hjetaniemi – Isle of Tulkila – Fishing by torchlight – Appearance of the Country towards the Arctic – Ofver Torneå – Adventure that befel the Author – Plants – Conflagration of the Forests – Havoc made by Wild Beasts – Kattila Cataracts – Passage of the Polar Circle – Scenery of the Frigid Zone – Breed of Cows – Tavonico – Beautiful Isles – Svansten – Mosquitos – their providential utility – Hirvas Koski – Pello – Skïders – Scricfinni – Aquatic Birds – Diet of the Natives – Lapland Nectar – Checks in Population – Jarhonnen – Mode of killing Bears – Extraordinary

'Not So Barren or Uncultivated'

Prospect – Tugurium of the Laplanders – Junction of the Torneå *and* Muonio *Rivers.*

Beautiful variety of Spar – *Fruit of the* Rubus Chamæmorus – *Reception at* Kilpala – *Primeval Plough* – *Wooden Lock and Key* – Tervola – *Midnight Fishery at* Tivan-koski *Cataract* – Alaparkyla – *Rovila* – *Appearance of* Kiemi *Church* – Adelcrantz *the Peasant Architect* – *Dress of the Finlanders* – Kiemi *Fair* – *Sunday Ball at the Parsonage* – *Of the* Lapland *and* Finland *Languages* – *Universality of Superstitions respecting Sneezing* – Cypripedium bulbosum – *Haymaking in the Streets of* Torneå – *Visit to a Swedish Family* – *State of Natural History in Sweden* – *Curious example of the power of genius* – *Dinner given to the* Torneå *Merchants* – *Prevalence of Intoxication* – *Character of the* Finns – *Departure from* Torneå – *Extraordinary Refraction of the Atmosphere* – *Antient Fable of the Egg of Night* – *Uncultivated Fruits* – *Forest on Fire* – *Visit to the Minister* – *Departure from* Kiemi – *Difference discernible upon entering* Finland – Kjanfraniemi – Alafva – Ijo – Haukebodas – *Population and Agriculture* – Jukuri – *Arrival at* Uleåborg.

Chapter II
ULEÅBORG, IN OSTERO-BOTHNIA, TO UMEÅ
Signor Acerbi *and his Party* – *Interview with that Traveller* – *Colonel* Skiöldebrand – *National Music of* Finland – *North Cape* – *Baron* Silferhielm – *Generous behaviour of a Merchant* – *Trade of* Uleå – *Entertainment given by Baron* Silferhielm – *Animal Magnetism* – *Departure from* Uleåborg – *Plants* – *Mode of exhibiting the bodies of Criminals* – Brahestad – *Origin of the Court Uniform of Sweden* – *Appearance of the Country* – *Finland Fishermen* – *Description of Ostero-Bothnia* – *Beginning of the Rainy Season* – Gamla Carleby – *State of Literature* – Ny Carleby – Wasa – *Musical Instrument called* Hummer – *Passage of the* Quarken – *Isle of* Björkö – *Quay of the Natives* – *Village of* Björkö – *Inhabitants* – *their contempt of wealth* – *Male and Female Peasants* – *Population* – *Vegetable Productions* – *Voyage to* Umeå – *Antient Finnish* Rhune – *Popular* Swedish *Air* – *its Versification imitated in an* English *Ode*.

5 'Andrew Swinton'

The copies of Swinton's book in the Bodleian Library demonstrate the confusion which surrounds its authorship. In *Letters from Scan-*

dinavia (1796), published anonymously, 'by Mrs. Wollstonecraft' has been appended on the title page of both volumes, but this has been crossed out, with 'William Thomson' pencilled inside each front cover. In fact the book had appeared four years earlier as *Travels into Norway; Denmark, and Russia in the Years 1788, 1789, 1790 and 1791* 'by A. Swinton, Esq.' The attribution of Swinton's book to Thomson seems to be generally accepted, but on what basis I do not know. I think it likely that Thomson was not only prolific, but was also a 'ghost writer', who in this instance put together the reminiscences of a genuine traveller.

The *Annual Biography and Obituary* for 1818 opens with remarks on Thomson: 'This is one of the most extraordinary men of letters of the present age. His name with an exception to poetry, is connected with almost every species of composition, and it would be impossible to write the history of the literature of the reign of George III, without assigning him a place.' Among his literary achievements is listed the translation of Giuseppe Acerbi's *Travels throught Finland, Sweden, and Lapland to the North Cape in the Years 1798 and 1799,* one of the best-known works on Finland from this era.

An equally puzzling question is whether Thomson, or his source, ever went to Finland. He writes a good deal about the 'Finlanders', but none of the letters is addressed from Finland, nor does he mention any place in Finland. The letters are written from Ingria, which was then a 'St Petersburg Governorate' with a large Finnish-speaking population. (Wikipedia has an excellent history of Ingria.) If Thomson's descriptions and unfavourable opinions of the Finnish population were of much interest, I would have included him in the body of the book, but as they are not he gets only this notice in the Appendix. One paragraph will sufice to indicate Thomson's perplexing views; the 'Finlanders' are presumably those resident in Ingria, but perhaps those of 'Russian Finland':

> The poor Finlanders, tossed about from one master to another, hardly know to whom they belong: the Russians, as their conquerers, claim the superiority; and a Russian peasant, in comparison with the Finlander, deems himself a gentleman. The apparent slowness and stupidity of the Finlanders may be partly occasioned by a degrading treatment. My proposal of removing them to the province of the Ukraine, would put this numerous and industrious nation more on

a level with the Russians; and, if they actually possess abilities, a situation more independent will bring them forth. This plan would be of great service to the Russians. The contemplation of a people so much inferior to them, as the Finlanders are at present, leads them to suppose themselves more accomplished in manners and arts, than the world is yet willing to allow them to be.
(*Letters from Scandinavia.* II, 290.)

Notes and References

Epigraph: *The Critical Review: or, Annals of Literature* XL. 1775, p.36. Review of Wraxall's *Cursory Remarks*.

Introduction

Negative views of Finland:

> Tacitus, *A Treatise on the Situation, Manners, and Inhabitants of Germany.* (Warrington, 1777), 137.
> James, 216.
> Clarke, IX, 379.
> Carr, 193.
> Wraxall, 4.
> Clarke, XI, 261.
> Porter, 79.
> Swinton, II, 295.
> Wraxall, 196.

Interest in travelling north:

> Wraxall (1807), 3.
> Brooke (1823), [v].
> Turner, 53.
> Holmes, 17, 18.
> Carr, 4.
> Otter, 186–7.
> Marshall, I, ii.
> Consett, 147.
> Wollstonecraft, 109.
> Clarke's letter, 8 December 1799: Otter, 368. '[B]eyond Tornêa's lake,' Thomson had written, 'human nature just begins to dawn.' 'Winter' (1730 version), ll.887, 940. .

Lapland and the primitive:

> *The Comedy of Errors*, IV, iii. Marlowe's *Doctor Faustus* (I, i) has a reference to 'Lapland giants'. Fuseli's *Lapland Witches* is in the Metropolitan Museum, New York.

Clarke, IX, 504.

Porter, 299.

Keats, 'Epistle to John Hamilton Reynolds', l.46.

Barton, 150.

Gibbon, quoted by Clarke, IX, iv. Clarke (writing some fifty years after Gibbon) dismisses this belief as 'altogether chimerical'. (IX, vi.)

William Wordsworth, Preface to *Lyrical Ballads, with Other Poems* (1800).

The Seasons. The lines quoted are from 'Winter', ll.834–50.

The Spectator 336 (19 April) and 406 (16 June).

Consett, 60.

Herbert Hartman, 'Wordsworth's "Lapland Night".' *Review of English Studies* XIV (1938), 193.

The picturesque; the state of nature:

Definition from the National Gallery website.

Wraxall (1807), 207–8.

Coxe, 5.

Clarke, IX, 543. Clarke uses the term 'picturesque' nearly thirty times in his Scandinavian volumes.

Rousseau's ideas: Barton, 3. There is an interesting study of James Thomson's developing ideas of virtuous primitives in Chapter 3 ('The Golden Age') of *The Background of Thomson's 'Seasons'* by A. D. McKillop (University of Minnesots, 1942), 89–128.

Bowring, *The Westminster Review* xiv (April 1827), 323.

Consett, 85.

Lascelles: Introduction to Johnson's *A Journey to the Western Isles of Scotland*. Yale Edition, IX, xix.

Brooke (1827), 155–6, 535.

Clarke, X, 63; IX, 487.

Barton, 123.

Clarke, X, 561.

Borrow. See Hirn, 49–84 and Inge Kabell, 'George Borrow and Finland', *George Borrow Bulletin* 29.

Routes to and through Finland:

Great Coastal Road: information from Lauri Poropudas, 'The King's Road in Finland.' *The Posthorn*, May 2003.

Clarke's carriage: Otter, 370.

Pinkerton, 401.
Jones, 263.
Carr, 209.

Accommodation:
Coxe (1802), 8.
Clarke, XI, 355, 356.
Wraxall (1807) 211. On 'the closed coach' see Fjågesund and Symes, 46.
Norway: Rogan, 94.
Sweden: Barton, 50.
Elliott, 247.
Clarke, X, 62, 64; IX, 378.
Frankland, 43.
Monthly Magazine I (July 1827), 189.
William Mavor, *Historical Account of the Most Celebrated Voyages, Travels and Discoveries* . . . 25 volumes, 1796–1801. John Pinkerton, *A general Collection of the best and most interesting Voyages and Travels in all Parts of the World* . . . 17 volumes, 1808–14.
Edinburgh Review I (1802), 165.
Elliott, 369–70.

Joseph Marshall

I have chosen not to enter into any discussion about the authorship of Marshall's *Travels. The Monthly Review* 55 (1776), 430–1, admits to 'a violent suspicion that we have been conversing with a *non-entity*: and that the name of Squire Marshall [has] been assumed by some book-making genius, who might have good reasons, notwithstanding his *genius* for thinking any name better to go to market with, than his own.' The reviewer nonetheless quotes a statement that 'Mr. Marshall was a man of property; and that his estate lies at Budswell, in Northamptonshire.' This reviewer's conclusion seems reasonable: '. . . we observed in the news-papers, an account of the *death* of Joseph Marshall, Esq; Author of the Travels, &c. which account, if true, affords (as a grave writer expresses it) a strong assumption that he once lived.'

Marshall. Preface to Vol. 1, [i]–ii.
Vol. 3, 45, 46, 53, 47–8.
Vaasa: 54–68; Päijänne: 70–8; Savonlinna: 80.

Sir Nathaniel William Wraxall

For Wraxall's writings I have used both the first (1775) and fourth (1807) editions. The first contains many more harsh opinions, which are valuable because they presumably reflect more closely the views which the author held in 1774. The fourth softens many of these comments, but has so much new detail about Finland that it is in many places the more valuable version. I have ventured in a few places to use the 1807 paragraphing of longer 1775 passages.

> Mavor (1797), Vol. XVIII, [1]–2.
> Swinton, v.
> Wraxall (1775), 168. Wraxall has changed 'remain' in the 1775 edition to 'reside altogether' in 1807 (4–5; 185).
> Eckerö: (1807), 198, 199.
> Kastelholm: (1775), 188. East from Kastelholm: 191–4. The 'small islands' are given in 1807 as 'Wargate, Kumlinge, Brando, and Warsala'.
> Turku: 194–5; castle and cathedral: (1807) 210.
> Towards Helsinki: (1807) 211–13.
> From Helsinki: 213–18, 221.

William Coxe

> Barton, 15.
> Swinton, v–vi.

Quotations are taken from the first edition (1784) and the fifth (1802). The fourth edition (1792) was expanded to incorporate details of a second journey to northern Europe which Coxe had made in 1784–5, and adds accounts of Jutland, Norway, Livonia and Courland. The descriptions of Finland are revised stylistically, not with any obvious benefit; the only significant change is a description of Suomenlinna, which was in 1779 still work in progress. As with Wraxall, I have occasionally used the paragraphing of the later editions.

> Russian Finland: (1784) 70–2, 74, 75–7, 78–9.
> Swedish Finland: 79–82
> Suomenlinna: (1802) 15–16
> West of Helsinki: (1784) 84.
> Gulf of Bothnia: 85–90.

Matthew Consett

Edinburgh Review XIX (February 1812), 320.
Consett 'state of nature': 85; poetry: 63; Grot: 53.
Tornio: 53-4, 55, 56-7, 58-60; Laplanders' language and music: 62-3; religion and superstition: 64-6; Lapland skills: 68.
The Lapland girls: 153, 154, 156; Omai: Butler, 16; reindeer: Consett, 152; 'Ravensworth Castle and the Liddells' (publication of the Sunniside Local History Society.)

Edward Daniel Clarke

The first Scandinavian volume, describing northern Finland and Lapland, was published in 1819, and the second, describing Åland and southern Finland, posthumously in 1823. Quotations are from what may have been a uniform edition, dated 1824, where these volumes are designated as 'Part the Third, Scandinavia: Volume the Ninth, Tenth, and Eleventh'. The 1824 text, at least in the quoted passages, is unchanged, apart from a very few corrections of spelling.

Cripps and Malthus: Otter, 334, 337, 370, 371; Patricia James, xv. Otter describes his trip very briefly in his 'Memoir of Robert Malthus' prefixed to the 1836 edition of *Principles of Political Economy,* xxxvii.
Tornio to Enontekiö: Clarke IX, 336, 347-8. Otter, 352, 353.
Clarke, 359, 387, 368-9, 369-70, 378, 385-6; mosquitoes: *Edinburgh Review* I (1802), 170. Clarke, 404, 405, 406, 439, 368, 371, 426.
Enontekiö: 460, 470, 486-7, 489-91, 468, 471-2, 493-5; letter to Malthus, 9 July 1799: Otter, 355; Farewell: Clarke, 525.
After Enontekiö: 542-3; (*Gulliver's Travels* e.g. IV, iii). Clarke, 546-9, 559.
South from Roveniemi: Clarke X, 15, 19, 18, 20, 22, 23, 46.
Oulu and Ostrobothnia: 62, 64-5, 67, 68, 69, 70, 71-2, 75, 77, 81, 82.
Vaasa: 83, 84, 86, 87, 93.
Stockholm to Kumlinge: Otter, 374-5; Clarke XI, 175, 183, 188, 234, 197-8, 244, 246.
Kumlinge to Turku: 253-4, 259, 257, 258, 262; James Boswell, *Journal of a Tour to the Hebrides with Samuel Johnson,*

14 August, 1773; Clarke, 266, 267–8, 270.
Turku: 270, 271–2, 276–7, 285, 288–9; Otter, 382; Clarke, 343, 321, 326, 327, 293, 294, 336, 328–9; X, 79; XI, 340–1, 351.
West of Turku: 362, 364, 365, 365–6, 370, 371, 372, 373–4.

John Carr

Journey from Stockholm: [3], 181, 182, 184, 185, 188.
Turku: 190–2. The room where Carr stayed was undoubtedly the 'Seipellska salen' (Seipel Room); see Gardberg, 138. It is now a restaurant, *Linnankatu 3*.
Onwards to Russia: 193, 196, 200–3, 208–9, 210.

Sir Robert Ker Porter

R. D. Barnett, 'Robert Ker Porter: Regency Artist and Traveller', *Iran* x (1972) 19. *DNB*.
Vyborg to Turku: Porter, 298, 297, 300, 301.
West from Turku: 302–3, 304, 305–11; Avå: 312–13; Torsholma: 314–15; Kumlinge: 315–20; Eckerö, Signildsskä: 322–4; Porter's later history: *DNB*.

John Thomas James

Stockholm to Turku: 210–17; Helsinki: 218–22; 'a general view': 216; East of Helsinki: 223–4.

George Green

Preface, iv; 'Louisa' to 'Helsingforth': 164–5; post-house: 165; I cannot identify Welliosei. Turku–Vartsala: 167–8.

Robert Pinkerton

West to Porvoo: 396–7, 398–9, 399.
Porvoo to Somero: 401–2, 404; Turku: 405–6.

John Paterson

Biographical details from Alexander's Prefatory Memoir, esp. xix, xx.

Paterson, 270, 91, 140, 146.
1812 journey: 159, 163; 'translating and printing': *DNB*.
1814 journey: 218–19, 220.
1817 journey: 269–70, 271, 272–3, 275; Imatra: 241, 242, 243.
1819 journey: 321, 324–25.

Sir John Bowring

There is a good deal of information about Bowring in my article 'John Bowring and Finland', *Neuphilologische Mitteilungen* LXXV, 3 (1974), 428–43.

Exeter: *DNB*.
Thomas Hood, 'Sir John Bowring'. *Poetical Works* (Oxford, 1906), 666.
'Songs of the People': *Minor Morals* II (1835), 262–3. Bowring describes a song he heard 'once, when in the woods of Finland' (260–1).
Bowring, 125–6, 127–8, 129–30.
The reference to Don Juan is the Canto 2 of Byron's poem, where after a shipwreck the survivors in a boat resort to cannibalism.
Letter to Borrow, 26 January 1834 in W. I. Knapp, *Life . . . of George Borrow* (1899) I, 198.

Francis Bayley

The manuscript is in the Bodleian Library, Oxford; I have benefited from an annotated transcript made by L. Clark. Biographical material is from Clark's Introduction. All extracts are taken from his transcript.

George Matthew Jones

Vol. I, [ix]–x, xi– xii.
Stockholm to Turku: 248, 247, 250, 251, 250; Barrow, 146.
Turku: Jones, 255, 256–7, 260, 258, 260.
West from Turku: 261, 262–4, 267–9, 271–2,
West from Helsinki: 272–3, 274, 275–6, 266–9, 273, 275, 276.
Political reflections: 266–7.

Arthur de Capell Brooke

(1826) 512, 515, 517–18, 516, 534–5, 522–3, 528, 552.

Capt. James Edward Alexander

253–4, 255–7, 258–9, 259–60, 260–1, 262.

Capt. Charles Colville Frankland, RN

Travels to and from Constantinople (second edition, 1829) II, 177.
Frankland, iv, 3, 57, 71, 86, 89, 92, 93.
Turku: 95, 94; Ringbom, 268; Frankland, 96, 97–8, 98–9.
West from Turku: 101, 102, 106, 108–10, 111, 112, 113.

Charles Boileau Elliott

vi, 251; Murray's *Handbook* (1849), 352; Elliott, 248–9, 255–6,
257–8, 260, 261, 262, 250–1; Tacitus: 251 (Aiken's translation,
with one phrase altered.)
Comparative studies: 81, 251, 250; hair: 259–60.
English reticence: 254–5. The quotation is based on Shakespeare's
1 Henry IV, I, iii.

John Barrow

Quarterly Review LI (1834), 456–67.
Detail from the *ODNB*.
Preface, [i], 129–30, 131, 133, 138, 134–5, 129–30, 137, 138.
Turku: 140, 144, 141–3, 145–6, 146.

Charlotte Disbrowe

30–1.

The Marchioness of Westminster

Preface, 121, 131, 132, 133, 134.

Bibliography

All books published in London, unless otherwise stated.

Primary sources

Alexander, Capt. James Edward, *Travels to the Seat of the War in the East, through Russia and the Crimea, in 1829. With Sketches of the Imperial Fleet and Army, Personal Adventures, and Characteristic Anecdotes*. Vol. II. 1830.

Barrow, John Junr., *Excursions in the North of Europe, through Parts of Russia, Finland, Sweden, Denmark, and Norway, in the Years 1830 and 1833*. 1834.

Bayley, Francis, *The Travel Diary of Francis Bayley, 1823-4*. Ed. L. Clark. [1961.] Manuscript and typescript in the Bodleian Library, Oxford.

Bowring, John, *Autobiographical Recollections of Sir John Bowring. With a Brief Memoir by Lewin B. Bowring*. 1877.

Brooke, A. de Capell, *Travels through Sweden, Norway & Finmark to the North Cape. In the Summer of 1820*. 1823.

– *A Winter in Lapland and Sweden*. 1827.

Carr, John, *A Northern Summer; or Travels round the Baltic, through Denmark, Sweden, Russia, Prussia and Part of Germany, in the Year 1804*. 1805.

Clarke, Edward Daniel, *Travels in Various Countries of Europe, Asia and Africa. Part the Third: Scandinavia*. Vols. IX, X and XI. 1824.

Consett, Matthew, *A Tour through Sweden, Swedish Lapland, Finland and Denmark. In a Series of Letters*. Stockton, 1789.

Coxe, William, *Travels into Poland, Russia, Sweden, and Denmark*. Dublin, 1784. Vol. III.

– *Travels in Poland, Russia, Sweden and Denmark*. Fifth Edition, 1802. Vol. IV.

Disbrowe, Charlotte, *Original Letters from Russia*. 1878.

Elliott, Charles Boileau, *Letters from the North of Europe; or*

a Journal of Travels in Holland, Denmark, Norway, Sweden,
Finland, Russia, Prussia and Saxony. 1832.

Frankland, Captain C. Colville, RN, *Narrative of a Visit to the
Courts of Russia and Sweden, in the Years 1830 and 1832.* 1832,
Vol. I.

Green, George, *An Original Journal from London to St. Petersburgh,
by Way of Sweden.* 1813.

James, John Thomas, *Journal of a Tour in Germany, Sweden, Russia,
Poland, during the Years 1813 and 1814.* Vol. I. 1816.

Jones, George Matthew, RN, *Travels in Norway, Sweden, Finland,
Russia, and Turkey.* 1827. Vol. I.

Marshall, Joseph, *Travels through Holland, Flanders, Germany,
Denmark, Sweden, Lapland, Russia, the Ukraine, and Poland in
the Years 1768, 1769, and 1770.* 1772. Vols. I, III.

Mavor, William, *Historical Account of the most celebrated
Voyages, Travels, and Discoveries, from the Time of Columbus to
the Present Period.* Vol. XVII. 1797.

Otter, William, *The Life and Remains of Edward Daniel Clarke;
Professor of Mineralogy in the University of Cambridge.* 1824.

Paterson, John, *The Book for Every Land: Reminiscences of Labour
and Adventure in the Work of Bible Circulation in the North of
Europe and in Russia.* Edited with a Prefatory Memoir, by W. L.
Alexander. 1858.

Pinkerton, John, *A General Collection of the Best and Most
Interesting Voyages and Travels in all Parts of the World.* 1808–14.

Pinkerton, Robert, *Russia: or, Miscellaneous Observations on the
Past and Present State of that Country and its Inhabitants.
Compiled from Notes made on the Spot, during Travels, at
different Times, in the Service of the Bible Society, and a Residence
of Many Years in that Country.* 1833.

Porter, Robert Ker, *Travelling Sketches in Russia and Sweden during
the Years 1805, 1806, 1807, 1808.* Second Edition, 1813. Vol. II.

Swinton, Andrew (pseud. for William Thompson), *Travels into
Norway, Denmark and Russia in the Years 1788, 1789, 1790,
and 1791.* 1792. (Published also anonymously as *Letters from
Scandinavia, on the Past and Present State of the Northern
Nations of Europe.* 1796.)

Westminster, Marchioness of (Grosvenor, Elizabeth Mary), *Diary of
a Tour in Sweden, Norway, and Russia, with Letters.* 1879.

[Whatley, Thomas Denman], *Handbook for Northern Europe; Part II; Finland and Russia.* 1839.

Wollstonecraft, Mary, *Letters written in Sweden, Norway, and Denmark.* 1796. Ed. Brekke and Mee; Oxford (World's Classics) 2009.

Wraxall, Sir Nathaniel William, Bart., *Cursory Remarks made in a Tour through some of the Northern Parts of Europe, particularly Copenhagen, Stockholm and Petersburg.* 1775.

– *A Tour Round the Baltic, thro' the Northern Countries of Europe, particularly Denmark, Sweden, Finland, Russia & Prussia; In a Series of Letters.* 4th edition Corrected and Augmented. 1807.

Secondary sources

Dictionary of National Biography (1885–1900) (*DNB*)
Oxford Dictionary of National Biography (2004) (*ODNB*)

Barton, H. Arnold, *Northern Arcadia: Foreign Travelers in Scandinavia, 1765–1815.* Carbondale: Southern Illinois Press, 1998.

Butler, Marilyn, *Romantics, Rebels, and Reactionaries: English Literature and its Background 1760–1830.* Oxford, 1981.

Fjågesund, Peter, and Symes, Ruth A., *The Northern Utopia. British Perceptions of Norway in the Nineteenth Century.* Amsterdam/New York. 2003.

Gardberg, Carl-Rudulf. 'Brittiska Resenärer i Åbo 1804–1827.' In *Festskrift tillägnad K. Rob.V. Wikman,* Åbo, 1966.

Hirn, Yrjö, *Lärt Folk och Landstrykare i det Finska Finlands Kulturliv.* Helsingfors, 1939.

Holmes, Richard, Introduction to Mary Wollstonecraft, *A Short Residence in Sweden, Norway and Denmark.* Harmondsworth, Penguin, 1987.

James, Patricia (ed.), *The Travel Diaries of T. R. Malthus.* Cambridge, 1966.

Lascelles, Mary (ed.), Samuel Johnson, *A Journey to the Western Islands of Scotland.* Yale Edition of the Works of Samuel Johnson, ix. Yale University Press, 1971.

Ringbom, Åsa, *Societetshusen i Storfurstendömet Finland.* Helsingfors, 1988.

Rogan, Bjarne, 'From a Haven for Travellers to a Boarding House for Tourists: The Vicarage in the History of Travelling and Hospitality in Norway.' In Marie Wells (ed.), *The Discovery of Nineteenth-Century Scandinavia* (Norvik Press, 2008), 83–96.

Turner, Katherine, *British Travel Writers in Europe, 1750–1800: Authorship, Gender, and National Identity.* Aldershot: Ashgate. 2001.